USEFUL WOODTURNING PROJECTS

The best from **WOODTURNING** magazine

USEFUL WOODTURNING PROJECTS

The best from **WOODTURNING** magazine

GUILD OF MASTER CRAFTSMAN PUBLICATIONS LTD

This collection first published in 1995 by
Guild of Master Craftsman Publications Ltd,
Castle Place, 166 High Street, Lewes, East Sussex BN7 1XU

Reprinted 1996

ISBN 0 946819 807

Printed and bound in Great Britain by the
University Press, Cambridge

Front cover photograph by Tom Crabb

CONTENTS

NOTES

Please note that names, addresses, prices etc. were correct at the time the articles were originally published, but may since have changed.

Measurements: Cautionary Note

Throughout the book instances will be found where a metric measurement has fractionally varying imperial equivalents, usually within $^1/_{16}$in either way. This is because in each particular case the closest imperial equivalent has been given. For this reason it is recommended, particularly on the smaller projects, that a drawing is made of the work to ensure that the measurements have not lost anything in translation.

Also, although the measurements given here are carefully calculated and are accurate, some variation may occur when pieces are hand turned, so care must be taken and adjustment may be necessary as the work progresses.

A mixture of metric and imperial measurements should NEVER be used – always use either one or the other.

INTRODUCTION

What a fantastic success *Woodturning* magazine has turned out to be. Each month brings a new batch of readers, and with them come increasing demands for back issues so they can catch up on all the good things they have missed.

Unfortunately, this demand has outstripped the supply, and so, sadly, many back issues are now out of print and no longer available.

This new volume, in which we have collected together some of the very best project articles from the first 27 issues of *Woodturning* magazine, is in part a response to the demand for previously published articles.

Here you will find a whole range of useful project ideas – some quite basic, others more advanced – to keep woodturning enthusiasts busy for many happy hours.

This is the second of a series of books drawing on articles from back issues of *Woodturning*. The first, on techniques, was published last year, and others, including a further projects book, will surely follow.

There is a treasure trove of ideas, information and inspiration specifically designed for woodturners – articles by talented, expert authors which have graced the pages of *Woodturning* magazine from the very first issue in 1990. Whether you are looking for advice and tips on basic techniques, projects to try in your own workshop, or features on the most innovative artists and their work as a source of fresh inspiration, you can be sure you will find something to interest you in this series of books.

I hope you will enjoy reading – and making – the projects in this book, and that it, together with the magazine, will continue to provide you with inspiration for many years to come.

Nick Hough
Editor, *Woodturning*

Either-way Tray, hard maple
255mm x 230mm x 32mm 10″ x
9″ x 1¼″.

TURNING TRAYS

TOM CRABB

Whenever Tom Crabb starts cleaning his workshop, he finds offcuts too big to throw away. Playing around with these on the lathe has led to him turning thin and individualistic trays. Here he describes how to make them.

Tom Crabb learned woodworking as a boatbuilder in a small yard where everybody learned everything about building wooden boats.

To level out the ups and downs of the boatbuilding business he began writing how-to articles for woodworking magazines.

This has lead to the publication of over 20 articles and two books, *Making Wooded Boxes with the Band Saw*, and *Band Saw Projects*.

Tom lives in Richmond, Virginia and works full time designing and engineering furniture and point of purchase displays. He got his first lathe for Christmas in 1991 and now most of his spare time is spent in his shop, turning everything he can think of.

Many of my projects start with the intention of cleaning the workshop. That's how it was one day as I surveyed a corner filled with offcuts, butt ends of boards too big to throw away.

I chucked a piece about 150mm 6″ square and 38mm 1½″ thick to the lathe and began working it like a bowl. The corners were the rim of the bowl and the sides fell away to the straight edges. After some turning, a pleasing shape emerged.

Turning was bumpy at the corners and the edges were fairly ragged. This, I thought, would be easily dealt with on a belt sander.

I continued to work the piece thinner and thinner. When it was about 6mm ¼″ thick the outside corners begin to vibrate

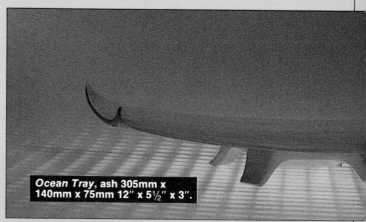

Ocean Tray, ash 305mm x 140mm x 75mm 12″ x 5½″ x 3″.

in a pattern with the chisel.

I tried steadying the piece with my hand but it still vibrated, my hand was getting hot and the corners kept whacking my thumb. I took it off the lathe and put it with other turning projects needing more thought.

After reading Vic Wood's article *Making a Square Edged*

Lidded Container, **Woodturning**, Autumn 1990. I retrieved my original idea.

But this time I surrounded a 150mm 6″ square x 25mm 1″ thick piece of red oak with waste wood and sawed out a circle (FIG 1), leaving 25mm 1″ of waste wood past the corners. I turned a slightly curved tray less than 1mm ³⁄₆₄″ thick inside

FIG 1

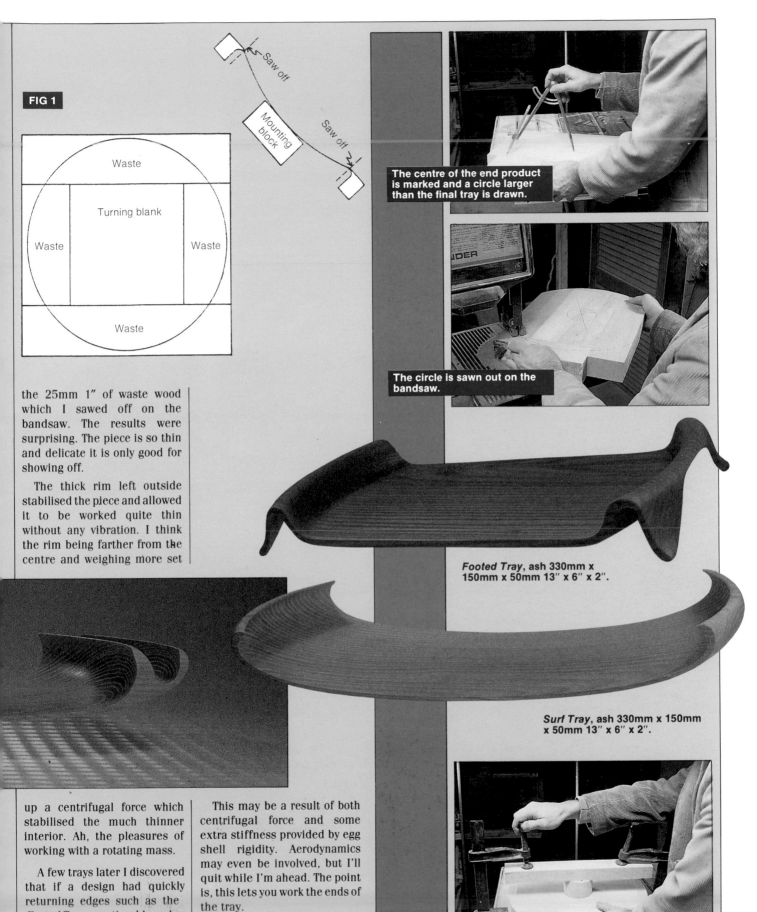

	Waste	
Waste	Turning blank	Waste
	Waste	

Saw off

Mounting block

Saw off

The centre of the end product is marked and a circle larger than the final tray is drawn.

The circle is sawn out on the bandsaw.

Footed Tray, ash 330mm x 150mm x 50mm 13" x 6" x 2".

Surf Tray, ash 330mm x 150mm x 50mm 13" x 6" x 2".

Gluing a mounting block in the marked centre for the faceplate.

the 25mm 1″ of waste wood which I sawed off on the bandsaw. The results were surprising. The piece is so thin and delicate it is only good for showing off.

The thick rim left outside stabilised the piece and allowed it to be worked quite thin without any vibration. I think the rim being farther from the centre and weighing more set up a centrifugal force which stabilised the much thinner interior. Ah, the pleasures of working with a rotating mass.

A few trays later I discovered that if a design had quickly returning edges such as the *Footed Tray*, or noticeable rocker in its shape, like the *Surf* and *Ocean* trays, the stabilising effect was the same.

This may be a result of both centrifugal force and some extra stiffness provided by egg shell rigidity. Aerodynamics may even be involved, but I'll quit while I'm ahead. The point is, this lets you work the ends of the tray.

Turning either type of tray begins by blocking in a turning blank with waste wood such as ▶

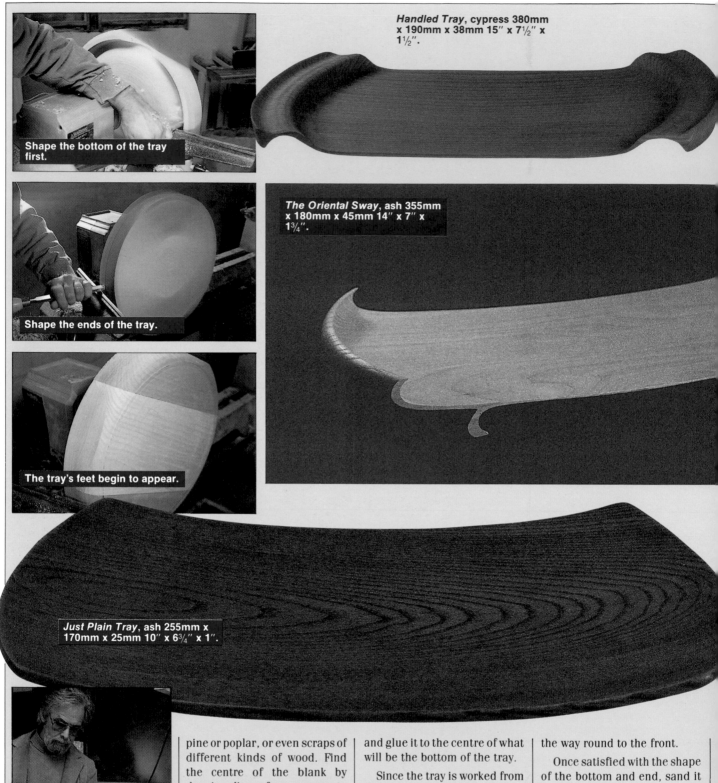

Shape the bottom of the tray first.

Handled Tray, cypress 380mm x 190mm x 38mm 15″ x 7½″ x 1½″.

Shape the ends of the tray.

The Oriental Sway, ash 355mm x 180mm x 45mm 14″ x 7″ x 1¾″.

The tray's feet begin to appear.

Just Plain Tray, ash 255mm x 170mm x 25mm 10″ x 6¾″ x 1″.

Work the inside of the tray, checking the thickness often.

pine or poplar, or even scraps of different kinds of wood. Find the centre of the blank by drawing lines from corner to corner. Use the centre to draw a circle larger than the turning blank and saw this out with a bandsaw.

Use another scrap of wood about 38-50mm 1½-2″ thick, with good gluing properties, to make a mounting block for your faceplate. Make the block a little larger than the faceplate

and glue it to the centre of what will be the bottom of the tray.

Since the tray is worked from the bottom, mounting the thickness of the spacer block will give you a little room to work between the lathe and the workpiece.

With the work mounted on the lathe and trued-up, begin shaping the bottom of the tray first. If you are working a tray where the end can be shaped, as in FIG 2, shape the end all

the way round to the front.

Once satisfied with the shape of the bottom and end, sand it to finish grade. This gives a fixed surface to measure from with the callipers.

Working on the lathe restricts your tool choices to scrapers, but you are not removing large amounts of wood and working from one mounting alleviates the possibility the piece will be out of plane or off centre when the mounting is reversed. Since

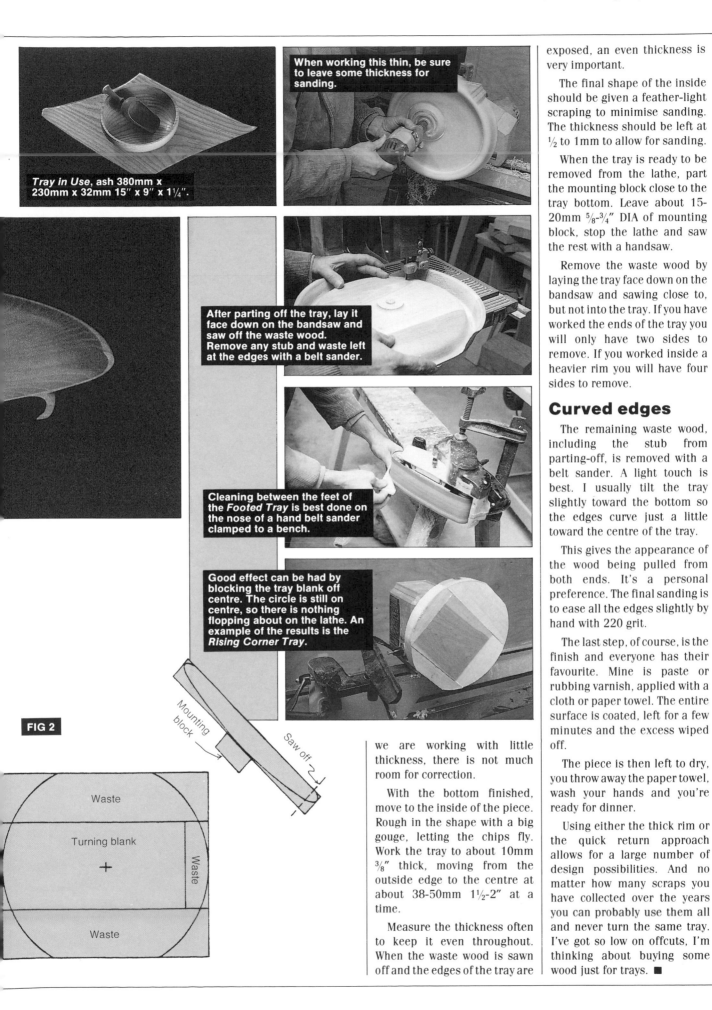

Tray in Use, ash 380mm x 230mm x 32mm 15" x 9" x 1¼".

When working this thin, be sure to leave some thickness for sanding.

After parting off the tray, lay it face down on the bandsaw and saw off the waste wood. Remove any stub and waste left at the edges with a belt sander.

Cleaning between the feet of the *Footed Tray* is best done on the nose of a hand belt sander clamped to a bench.

Good effect can be had by blocking the tray blank off centre. The circle is still on centre, so there is nothing flopping about on the lathe. An example of the results is the *Rising Corner Tray*.

FIG 2

Mounting block

Saw off

Waste

Turning blank

Waste

Waste

exposed, an even thickness is very important.

The final shape of the inside should be given a feather-light scraping to minimise sanding. The thickness should be left at ½ to 1mm to allow for sanding.

When the tray is ready to be removed from the lathe, part the mounting block close to the tray bottom. Leave about 15-20mm ⅝-¾" DIA of mounting block, stop the lathe and saw the rest with a handsaw.

Remove the waste wood by laying the tray face down on the bandsaw and sawing close to, but not into the tray. If you have worked the ends of the tray you will only have two sides to remove. If you worked inside a heavier rim you will have four sides to remove.

Curved edges

The remaining waste wood, including the stub from parting-off, is removed with a belt sander. A light touch is best. I usually tilt the tray slightly toward the bottom so the edges curve just a little toward the centre of the tray.

This gives the appearance of the wood being pulled from both ends. It's a personal preference. The final sanding is to ease all the edges slightly by hand with 220 grit.

The last step, of course, is the finish and everyone has their favourite. Mine is paste or rubbing varnish, applied with a cloth or paper towel. The entire surface is coated, left for a few minutes and the excess wiped off.

The piece is then left to dry, you throw away the paper towel, wash your hands and you're ready for dinner.

Using either the thick rim or the quick return approach allows for a large number of design possibilities. And no matter how many scraps you have collected over the years you can probably use them all and never turn the same tray. I've got so low on offcuts, I'm thinking about buying some wood just for trays. ∎

we are working with little thickness, there is not much room for correction.

With the bottom finished, move to the inside of the piece. Rough in the shape with a big gouge, letting the chips fly. Work the tray to about 10mm ⅜" thick, moving from the outside edge to the centre at about 38-50mm 1½-2" at a time.

Measure the thickness often to keep it even throughout. When the waste wood is sawn off and the edges of the tray are

Cyril Brown's interest in woodwork and the delights of sound, smell and feel of wood when working with hand tools especially, was kindled when he first entered the woodwork room of the Brunswick Junior Tech School in 1935.

Less than two years later, a week or so after his 14th birthday, he went to work as a lad labourer in a furniture factory for 6 shillings per week. That experience quickly extinguished his dream and he turned his back on the wood scene for 14 years.

After 5½ years in the RAN during WWII he acquired some basic tools and built his own first home over a period of 2½ years during weekends and holidays. For the next 28 years woodworking was a recreational pursuit, rebuilding and extending a further two homes, building boats and furniture for the family until he retired to live at Point Lonsdale, a seaside village resort some 105km from Melbourne.

Following another extensive rebuilding programme Cyril has had the time and the resolve to refine his limited skills and pursue new directions in wood and other crafts. He believes retirement gives the opportunity to do this, and to explore things he previously only thought about.

Cyril was a founding member and is currently secretary of a local woodworking group, the Queenscliff & District Woodworkers. His other interests include book collecting, reading and bookbinding.

Bookends for Beginners

CYRIL BROWN

When Cyril Brown wanted some simple but useful hand made gifts in a hurry he came up with these attractive bookends. They are easy to turn for the beginner, yet make ideal presents.

A year or so ago my wife and I planned to visit a few friends while holidaying in the northern states of New South Wales and Queensland, and stay with each of them for two or three days.

Believing it is nice to be able to acknowledge hospitality with some token of appreciation I thought on this occasion some hand-made bookends would be appropriate.

Time was a little short and I had already made up a couple of pairs of plain bookends which I had decorated with chip carving, but this was fairly time consuming. I needed another three pairs at least so I thought of turning them. The finished result can be seen in the photograph. This is how I went about the job.

I had a few smallish pieces which were offcuts from other jobs. They were Bollywood, which is easy to turn and carve, and Queensland Walnut which is not so easy to work but does finish nicely. The sketch will give an indication of the sizes I used but these are not critical. It depends on what size timber offcuts you may have, but if you settle on something about the dimensions indicated you will find the finished product a practical size.

Borrowing a technique used by that well-known Australian woodturner Vic Wood when he turns his square bowls and other objects, I glued on to the edges of the bookend material some scrap pine of the same thickness. First you have to square the joining edges and work out the appropriate sizes.

When the glue dries one side has to be surfaced so it can be fixed to the faceplate of your

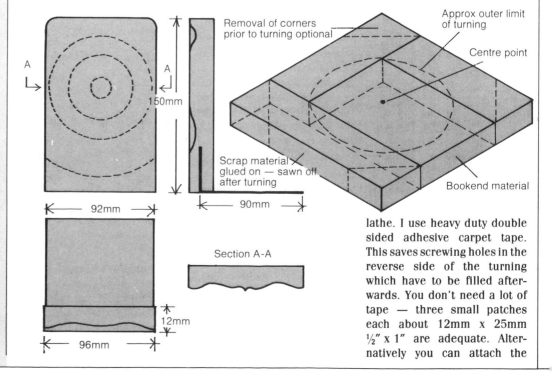

lathe. I use heavy duty double sided adhesive carpet tape. This saves screwing holes in the reverse side of the turning which have to be filled afterwards. You don't need a lot of tape — three small patches each about 12mm x 25mm ½″ x 1″ are adequate. Alternatively you can attach the

The fold is around 40mm 1⅝" from the end which leaves a projection of about 90mm 3½". Before fitting these angles to the ends saw 3mm ⅛" off the bottom of the inside leg of the wooden end to accommodate the thickness of the metal as well as the bend in the fold. Also smooth the edges of the plate with a file so they will not scratch the bookshelves or table, or the covers of the books.

To secure the metal supports in the bookends I put a dab of epoxy resin (Araldite) on the metal before inserting it into the slot. I then filled the edges of the saw cut with wood filler to match the colour of the wood.

As an alternative to using folded metal you could use a flat metal plate or 3mm ⅛" ply fixed into a recess cut in the bottom of the bookend, FIG 3. Use long countersunk screws for metal and nails and glue for ply.

These are only book supports and the end books hold the bookends in position so there is no great strain on the angle joints. Use whichever method seems easiest to you. You can apply your favourite finish — I used a satin varnish.

So there you are — a fairly easy project which doesn't take long to complete and a most useful gift to boot. The sets we gave away were greatly appreciated and, more importantly, are still in use. ∎

project material to a wooden faceplate with the time honoured paper sandwiched between.

You can now get on with the more exciting part, the actual turning which we all enjoy. You don't have to follow my pattern precisely. Have fun, do your own thing and create your own design. When you are satisfied with the design and you have smoothed the surface to your satisfaction, remove the piece from the faceplate and turn the other bookend likewise to make a pair. Use whatever tools you are comfortable with to achieve the desired result. If you are a scraper person that's fine, alternatively you might prefer a gouge.

After the pieces have been turned, saw off the scrap timber, plane up the edges and round the upper corners if you want to. It depends on whether the square corner leaves you with a fragile edge. I then cut the slot in the lower edge with a hand rip saw which gives a cut just wide enough (at least my hand saw does) to accommodate the 18 gauge sheet metal angle pieces which support the bookends in an upright position.

I got a sheet metal merchant to cut up the required number of metal support plates from 18 gauge galvanised sheet metal

around 130mm 5⅛" long but 5mm 3/16" less than the width of the wooden ends. Unless you have the means of folding the metal cleanly it is best to ask the merchant to do this for you because 18 gauge plate is about 1mm thick and pretty tough.

A sheet metal merchant or plumbers' merchant should have a metal folding machine, but if this is going to be expensive you can fold it yourself using the following method.

To Fold Sheet Metal

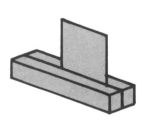

FIG 1.

Clamp the short end of the metal between two squared pieces of hardwood in G cramps or a metalwork vice FIG 1. Use another piece of hardwood about 75-100mm 3-4" long by 25-38mm 1-1½" thick. Place this piece on the edge of the front piece of wood in the vice and with both hands push and

fold the protruding metal flap over and then hammer it flat to get a sharp angle FIG 2. You could use brass which is softer and easier to fold.

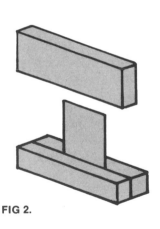

FIG 2.

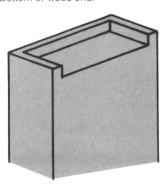

Bottom of wood end.

FIG 3.

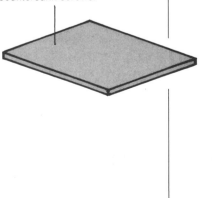

Use 3mm ply — glue and nail or a flat metal plate with long countersunk screws.

PUT A LID ON IT

ERNIE CONOVER

By fitting a turned lid to a quality bottle you can make someone a nice present, do your bit for conservation — and save a bob or two, says Ernie.

Ernie Conover is our contributing editor in America. He teaches woodworking in general, and woodturning in particular, at Conover Workshops, a school he and his wife Susan operate together. In addition to writing and lecturing widely, he is a technical consultant to a number of companies on design and manufacture of woodworking tools and machines.

I can't help it. Every time I throw away a nice looking bottle, my Scottish ancestry gets the better of me. I am not talking about fizzy drinks or mayonnaise bottles, I am talking about the classy ones you receive at Christmas and for birthdays,

the kind premium marmalades, jellies, mustards or whiskies are packed in.

My family surreptitiously remove such bottles from the house lest Pack Rat Ernie should claim them.

Little do they know that I have another way to glean

them. Our town has an active recycling programme, and I have acquired the task of hauling bottles down to the recycling centres, where I take out the good ones.

These bottles often have no advertising in the glass and the paper labels can be easily

steamed off. The lid is a different matter.

More often that not it is a litany of logos, claims and testimonials about the product, making the bottle good for holding polish or nails, but is not something you would give at Christmas — unless you are a Scot that is.

Most discount store canisters, tea caddies and storage containers also have mediocre, if not tacky, lids. An otherwise nice container will have a chromed, stamped steel lid, or even worse, plastic.

My solution to the above problems is to turn a lid. Not only is this a splendid turning exercise, but you make treasure from trash.

Facade

While sometimes I turn a new lid entirely of wood for a container, at other times I embed the metal cap in wood. It's a facade but it works.

I thought I would take a look at making lids for such bottles and in the process look at some commercial and home made chucks.

> "I am beginning to feel a bit like Don Quixote tilting at windmills."

Lids are usually face work and interesting wood really makes them look special. If the wood stands up to a bit of water and comes back smiling, all the better. Common North American woods I use regularly for lids are cherry and maple. In the UK beech or elm would work nicely. For jars I give on special occasions I use maple burl.

Woodturning readers know well my views on chucks. I think a home made one is superior to one you buy. I must admit, however, that of late I am beginning to feel a bit like Don Quixote tilting at windmills.

Most people listen to my arguments for home made chucks thoughtfully, then go out and buy the metal variety.

I have many ideas why this is so, but my purpose is not to comment on current culture but to turn some jar lids.

Therefore, I thought I would take a close look at the features and capabilities of four-jaw scroll chucks. For this article I obtained a OneWay Chuck, with all the bells and whistles. The OneWay is made in Stratford, Ontario, Canada, and closely follows the pattern established by the Nova Chuck which is made in New Zealand. Since I already own a Nova it was easy to make direct comparisons.

Both chucks have 100mm 4" DIA bodies that enclose the scroll plate and have keyways for the four jaws. The scroll is not more than a plate with a spiral milled into the surface.

It can be thought of as a screw thread on a flat plate, a screw thread in one dimension. Levers inserted into the two halves of the body turn the scroll plate.

The jaws have matching ridges that engage the scroll thread. The main jaws are numbered and must be inserted in the matching keyways in numerical order for the chuck to close on centre.

Jaw one is inserted and the scroll is turned until it engages it, then number two and so on.

"Not only is this a splendid turning exercise, but you make treasure from trash."

The jaws now go in and out in unison, controlled by the position of the scroll plate.

From a working standpoint there is not much difference between the two chucks, save one. The OneWay is a safety chuck. The one great danger with a scroll chuck is over-extending the jaws.

If the scroll loses its hold on one or more jaws, it will fly out of the chuck body when the lathe is started, with possibly horrific results.

A good rule of thumb with any scroll chuck is to never extend the jaws more than half way out of the body, for this insures that the scroll plate maintains a secure hold on all the jaws.

Safety

The OneWay has a pin in the jaws that engages the body of the chuck and prevents them from being over extended. This is a noteworthy safety feature, especially if young people or Sunday turners are to use the chuck.

Ernie must have a very early Nova Chuck, for current models have a stop screw fitted to ensure the jaws cannot be over-extended. The Nova is therefore a safety chuck. Ernie should carry out a modification or contact the New Zealand manufacturers — Ed.

Both chucks sport top jaw, in a variety of configurations, that bolt to the main jaws with socket head cap screws. While Nova simply provides a right angle hex key for this task, OneWay furnishes a Tee handle hex wrench. While some turners use standard metalworking chucks for woodturning, they tend not to work out well. The contact area of the jaws is too

small to hold well in wood.

Therefore both of our test chucks sport top jaws with much greater radial contact area. The trick is to pick a set of jaws with a grip diameter that is as close as possible to what you wish to hold.

I have tried to convince the OneWay folks to offer blank plastic jaws which could then be scraped to any desired configuration. This is a common practice in the metal working industry. Soft jaws are also more accurate than the standard jaws for they are true to your lathe.

Nylon/plastic jaws are available in the UK from the Midland Tool Manufacturing Co, Unit 4, Belle Eau Park, Bilsthorpe, Newark, Notts NG2 2TX. Tel: 0623 870411 — Ed.

If one of the three available sets of jaws won't work, there are large flat aluminium sectors with taped holes in concentric circles on their faces. Together these form a large flat aluminium plate with concentric bolt circles.

Dovetail-shaped rubber bumpers with steel bushings in the centres, what I call rubber baby bumpers after the children's tongue twister, mount in the holes.

The rubber baby bumpers are far better on the OneWay than on the Nova, but I have an early prototype of the Nova plate jaws, so they may have been improved.

Both chucks come with a heavy screw that may be gripped in the jaws, effectively turning them into screw chucks. In the following photos and captions on turning jar lids I have tried to use a variety of jaws to show the chucks capabilities. ▶

Cherry lid for canister jar

Photo 1. The blank for this lid is too big for any of the three sets of jaws. While it could be gripped by rubber baby bumpers on the sector jaws another alternative is a home made pressure-turning chuck. This is simply a nail in the centre of a glue block. The nail is filed to a point that protrudes about 1.5mm ¹⁄₁₆″ proud of the block.

Photo 2. A small block between the live centre and the work prevents the centre from marking and allows the centre position to adjust itself as the work is seated on the nail by the tailstock ram.

Photo 3. Scraping a dovetail-shaped recess for the chuck to expand into.

Photo 4. Expanding the chuck into the freshly scraped pocket.

Photo 5. The partially completed lid with the inside recess scraped to match the original lid on the right.

Photo 6. Changing to a set of jaws with a larger grip range for gripping the inside of the partially completed lid.

Photo 7. Expanding the chuck into the inside recess of the lid.

Photo 8. The completed lid.

Photo 9. The completed lid with the chuck.

Photo 10. Mounting the screw that turns the OneWay (or the Nova) into a screw chuck.

Cookie jar lid

My friend and fellow turner, Palmer Sharpless, gave my wife and I a mammoth clay cookie jar last summer. It was made by his daughter Linda, a professional potter from Spruce Pine, North Carolina.

When we called Palmer to thank him he warned us: "The problem with that jar is the lid. You can't steal cookies without someone hearing the clay lid open. What you have to do is turn a good quiet wood replacement."

This is a case where the peculiar holding needs of the reverse side of the cookie jar lid was better suited to jam chucking than the scroll chucks. ▶

The best laid plans of mice and men often go astray, and so it was with my new stealth lid. My parrot's cage is in the kitchen and she loves cookies — even more than I do. A robber baron at heart, she snitches if I don't pay tribute. Unless I share some of my ill-gotten gains with her, she makes such a racket that even the neighbours know what I am up to.

Photo 11. To drill a hole for mounting on the screw chuck it is helpful to first get a firm bite on the blank with a bench dog.

Photo 12. Making a jam chuck to catch the knob of the partially completed cookie jar lid.

Photo 13. Chalking the chuck with blackboard chalk to make it grip better.

Photo 14. Turning the underside of the lid while it is held in the jam chuck.

Photo 15. Removing the completed lid from the jam chuck.

Photo 16. The completed wood lid and the old ceramic lid next to the jam chuck.

Turning a wood facade

Photo 17. For the jaws to be accurate it is imperative to remove all chips and dirt with an old paint brush.

Photo 18. The aluminium sectors and rubber baby bumpers with the blank for the facade mounted.

Photo 19. After facing and turning a foot on the blank the jaws are changed and the work is reversed. Chucking is by compression on the foot.

Photo 20. Trial fit of the lid in the earlier turned recess.

Photo 21. The completed recess and the old metal lid.

Photo 22. Adding chatter work to the nearly completed lid. Although chatter work is best on end grain the random nature of this burl lends itself to the technique.

Photo 23. The completed lid on the jar.

Photo 24. The completed cookie jar lid, canister lid, bayonet jar lid and two mustard jars. The lid on the left mustard jar was chip carved by my friend Wayne Barton.

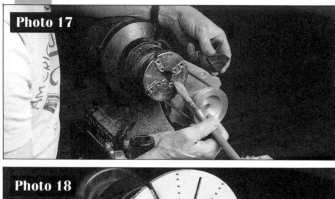
Photo 17

Photo 18

Photo 19

Photo 20

Photo 21

Photo 22

Photo 23

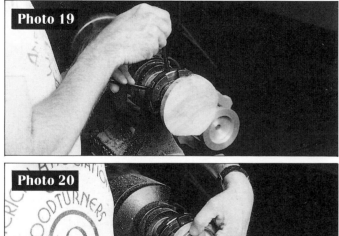
Photo 24

CONCLUSION

Although I am not about to give up jam chucking I have now ameliorated my stand on metal chucks. The Nova and the OneWay offer a vast improvement over what has been available to date in a woodturning chuck.

They are straight forward and easily understandable without having to revert to the directions after any period of disuse. Most of the collet chucks require an engineering degree to figure out, so this is a welcome development.

While any turner can benefit from them they are most appealing for the occasional turner or beginners who do not possess sufficient turning skills to jam chuck. My only reservation to the chucks is the cost — but then, I am a Scot. ∎

AN EGGSTRAORDINARY COLLECTION

A. J. M. CATHRO

James Hislop was a professional woodturner in Pitlochry, Scotland, until he died last year. He had a passion for collecting different woods, which he turned into eggs. Here a friend describes Hislop's work.

The late James A. Hislop was a professional woodturner with a lifelong interest in his raw material. Over the years he made a collection of eggs turned from hard and soft woods from South-east Asia, Southern, West and East Africa, Australia and Central and South America.

In all he made more than 500 eggs, of which 240 were housed in a special display cabinet.

Colour

His purpose in showing the various species of wood in egg form was to bring out the colour and grain features of the timber to the best advantage. For this reason he included several eggs of the same species in the collection.

Those well acquainted with wood will be aware of the infinite variety in spalted beech, for example, or the emerald green streaks and blotches in spalted ash. But not everyone realises the vastly different appearance of an egg turned from the sawn trunk compared with the branch of the same tree. The branch wood is far more interesting because the annual rings are intact.

Jim also felt that buttress wood, usually left to rot in the forest after logging, was much neglected. Being of a different structure, it can give a very different type of grain from trunk or branch wood.

A strange story lies behind one specimen in the collection. It is a scarce Malayan hardwood (Nyereh Batu) which grows in mangrove swamps and was cut in 1939.

Jim, who was working in Malaya at the time, went off on war service leaving the timber in the hands of a local Chinaman. ▶

Jim Hislop with his wooden egg collection.

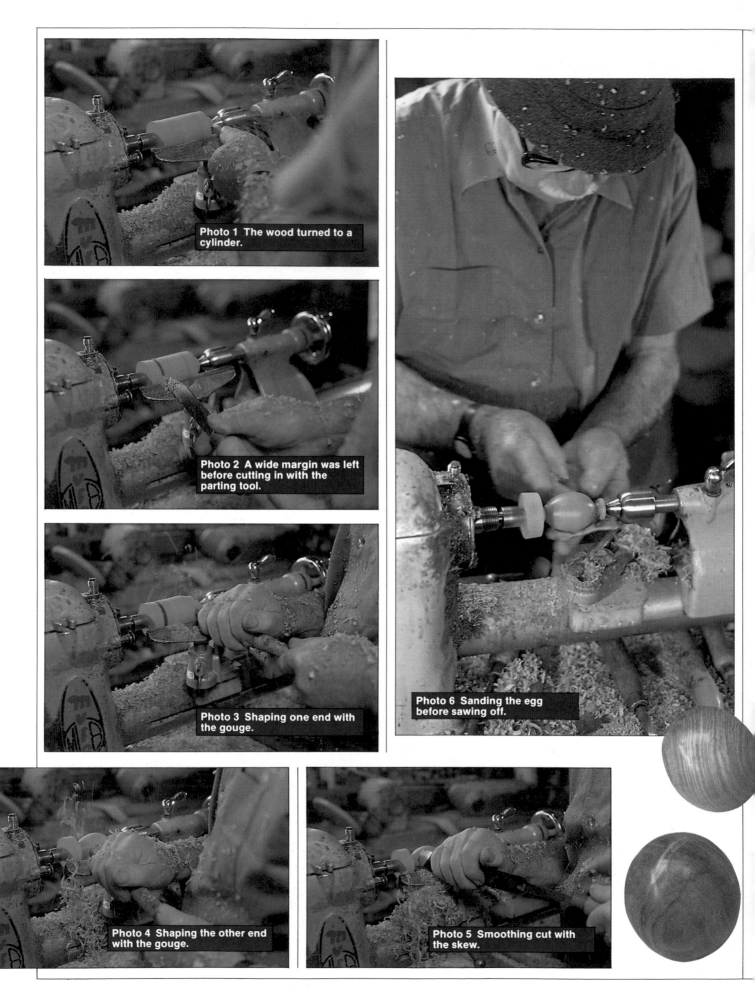

Photo 1 The wood turned to a cylinder.

Photo 2 A wide margin was left before cutting in with the parting tool.

Photo 3 Shaping one end with the gouge.

Photo 6 Sanding the egg before sawing off.

Photo 4 Shaping the other end with the gouge.

Photo 5 Smoothing cut with the skew.

Part of Jim Hislop's collection.

Eggs in a variety of woods.

Photos by
Alastair Gowans.

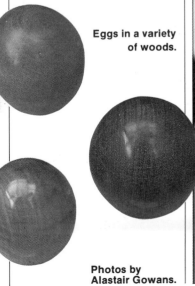

When he returned some five years later the man produced the timber which he had hidden from the Japanese at great personal risk, so this egg can truly be called a war-time souvenir.

The method Jim used to turn these eggs may bear little relation to that advocated or described by other expert woodturners, but the end result is generally quite acceptable.

Photo 7 Final sanding and buffing on the lathe.

This is the technique he demonstrated to me.

First he turned a piece of wood (in this case pink ivory) measuring 85mm 3½" x 50mm 2" square to a cylinder between centres (Photo 1).

The diameter at the tailstock end was reduced to leave a pin about 10mm ⅜" DIA to allow room for the finishing cut. A grooved parting tool was used to mark off the other end of the egg and cut in as far as prudent, depending on the strength of the wood involved and the judgment of the turner.

More wood was left at the headstock end than is usually necessary as there had to be sufficient to prevent the tool hitting metal and also to ensure that no marks were left on the finished article by the drive centre (Photo 2).

To save valuable and expensive wood a piece of scrap timber could be glued to either end of the blank before turning, thus utilising the full length of the precious wood.

Starting at the centre, one end of the egg was shaped using a spindle gouge. This tool was of slender section and took up little space when shaping either end (Photo 3).

Contours

Both ends were shaped with a gouge and skew (Photos 4 and 5). The grooved parting tool was also used on its side to follow the contours nicely and leave a fine finish.

Sanding was done with 100, 150 and 250 grit paper before the two ends were sawn off (Photo 6).

The rough ends were then sanded on a drum sander using fine grit belts, the last being a well-worn belt to smooth off any irregularities. Finally the ends were polished using mops on the lathe (Photo 7).

Finishing was with cellulose sanding sealer, French polish and wax, which when buffed produced a glass-like finish. ∎

SOLD ON CEDAR

BERLE MILLER

Yellow cedar is Berle Miller's favourite wood and, living in British Columbia, he is never short of supplies. Here he describes how to turn this beautiful wood into a tall dry-flower vase.

Many turners have their favourite woods and I am no exception. Living on Vancouver Island gives me a large supply of timbers to work with and one I have particular respect for is yellow cedar (chamaecyparus nootkatensis).

Here I describe how to make a tall dry-flower vase from this beautiful wood. A vase can be an attractive object in itself, as well as providing a holder for dry-flower arrangements.

I start with a billet that has been dried down to around 12% moisture content. It requires close examination for any cracks parallel to the long grain. The grain has to be parallel to the lathe bed.

Photo 1 Rive and select a billet for long grain woodturning.

Photo 1 shows a 125mm 5″ x 125mm 5″ x 405mm 16″ section which has been selected from a longer piece. Also, the timber has been riven, not sawn, to ensure I am working with the timber, not against it.

Photo 2 Mounting between centres — turn down the ends first.

When mounted between centres (Photo 2) the ends are cut down first, to search again for any cracks. Any that are found can be filled with the versatile cyanoacrylate adhesive (Photo 3).

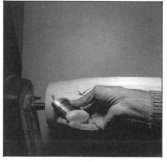

Photo 3 Apply cyanoacrylate glue for any cracks that may appear.

The tailstock end of the cylinder is trimmed off true (Photos 4 and 5). This end will be reversed and glued to a mounting block shown being made ready to receive a faceplate in Photos 6, 7 and 8.

Wood mounting blocks are

Photo 4 Cleaning off the end.

Photo 5 Ensure the cylinder end is true.

Photo 6 Preparing a wood mounting piece.

Photo 7 Fitting a recess for a faceplate.

Photo 8 Screwing the faceplate to the wood mounting piece.

hard to beat if you make the recess for an exact fit for the rim of the faceplates. Then you have a true lineup each time.

If the screw holes wear out, rotate the faceplate an inch or so for new holes. It is surprising how long you can keep using these mounting pieces.

In Photo 9 the faceplate is mounted on the headstock and a 3mm ⅛″ recess cut to receive the previously prepared cylinder. This keeps the cylinder from

Photo 9 After placing the faceplate on the headstock with a mounting piece previously turned, an accurate 3mm ⅛″ recess is cut to fit the cylinder shown in Photo 5.

sliding all over the place and getting out of alignment when gluing. A depth check ensures a good glue bond.

Titebond, or something similar, works well for this. Cyanoacrylate may also be used, but it is slightly too brittle for some of the stresses that will be placed upon this turning. It is also expensive.

The revolving tail centre is moved to the cylinder (Photo 10) and forces the piece in place. Fifteen minutes is usually long

Photo 10 Glue the cylinder into the recess using the tailstock as a clamp.

enough for it to become tacky.

Since only light cuts are to be made at this time for correcting any out-of-true roundness, you can proceed without delay. Photo 11 shows how an old 75mm 3″ x 535mm 21″ sanding belt can be used for smoothing.

Photo 11 Sanding method using 75mm 3″ x 535mm 21″ salvaged sanding belt.

These belts can be used for a long time because of their toughness and easy clean-up with a wire brush. Also, most of the dust ends up in a neat pile below the turning. Vacuum it up before it becomes airborne. Now allow the glue bond to cure for three or four hours.

Photo 12 Turning mounted with the steady rest and a recess cut for a bit.

Photo 13 A 2½″ bit entering the recess.

A steady rest (Photos 12 and 13) is mounted about three fourths of the way toward the tailstock. The one shown is a home made affair, as it is difficult to find a rest at a reasonable price. The detail ▶

Berle Miller was born in 1919 in Iowa County, Iowa. He has had a number of careers since gaining a degree in Industrial Arts Education — teacher, owner-manager of a millwork company, house builder and an associate in heavy and industrial contracting.
He retired in 1974 to the Beachcomber area of Nanoose Bay on Vancouver Island, British Columbia, where the forests, mountains and sea provide background material for experiments in wood. Art shows and galleries give him the chance to share his work with others. Berle works with a variety of materials and tools and is self-taught.
His work was featured on the cover and the Focus on Hidden Talent Worldwide feature in Issue 15 of *Woodturning*.
*Berle Miller,
R. 1. Box 32
Beachcomber,
Nanoose Bay, B.C.
Canada, VOR 2RO.*

FIG 1 **Steady rest.**

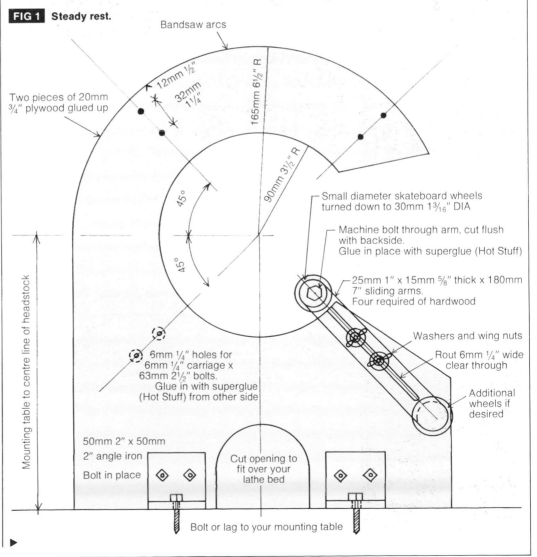

Bandsaw arcs

Two pieces of 20mm ¾″ plywood glued up

12mm ½″

32mm 1¼″

165mm 6½″ R

90mm 3½″ R

45°

45°

Mounting table to centre line of headstock

6mm ¼″ holes for 6mm ¼″ carriage x 63mm 2½″ bolts. Glue in with superglue (Hot Stuff) from other side

Small diameter skateboard wheels turned down to 30mm 1³/₁₆″ DIA

Machine bolt through arm, cut flush with backside. Glue in place with superglue (Hot Stuff)

25mm 1″ x 15mm ⅝″ thick x 180mm 7″ sliding arms. Four required of hardwood

Washers and wing nuts

Rout 6mm ¼″ wide clear through

Additional wheels if desired

50mm 2″ x 50mm 2″ angle iron

Bolt in place

Cut opening to fit over your lathe bed

Bolt or lag to your mounting table

shown in FIG 1 should provide the information to make one.

For woodturning, the 90 DEG four wheel system is more satisfactory than the 120 DEG three wheel system. With the forces being applied to a 3mm $\frac{1}{8}$" wall thickness turning, the wood flexes quite a bit.

Also, the lower two wheels cradle the piece while loosening the top two wheels for removing and replacing the turning. Alignment is maintained.

By cutting a 12mm $\frac{1}{2}$" to 20mm $\frac{3}{4}$" recess into the end grain to the exact outside diameter of the large bit used for drilling, you can be sure the true centre will be maintained. Most large bits wander if they are not started by a recess as in Photo 13.

Photo 14 Drilling to the depth of the short bit.

Run the lathe speed at 500 RPM or under for the drilling. First use the short shank bit as far as it will go (Photo 14). Now mount the bit into an extension (Photo 15 and FIG 2).

Photo 15 Extension for bit entering the work.

FIG 2 Simple bit extension.

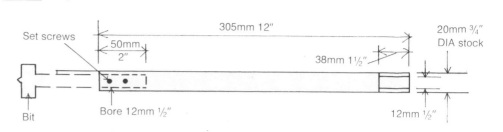

Grind a flat on drill bit for set screws

A mark on the extension bar indicates the depth of the hole. Nearing the final depth (Photo 16), keep the hole cleaned out with a vacuum (Photo 17).

Things get hot down this deep and invariably moisture will be evident.

Photo 16 Boring deeply with the extension bit.

Photo 17 Vacuum out all shavings.

It is essential to keep the bit sharp. End grain drilling dulls bit edges fast. My metalworking friend retempers these bits, and then grinding with abrasives is necessary to sharpen. Carbide tipped bits may be better.

After setting up a box (Photo 18 and FIG 3) straddling the lathe bed, a boring bar is brought into use. Guide blocks and a hold-down are aligned so the interior has the profile you have in mind (Photo 19).

Photo 18 Boring bar in use to finish contour the interior. Note angle on box support and guide blocks with hold down.

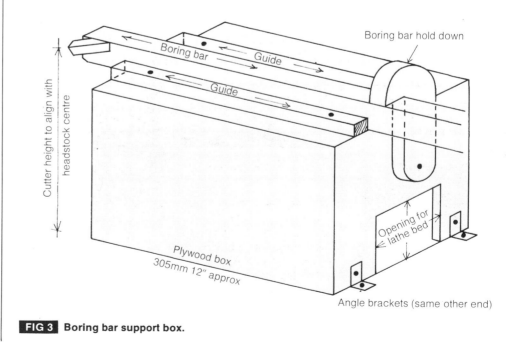

FIG 3 Boring bar support box.

Photo 19 Finished interior work is completed with a sanding drum on ¼" drill extension.

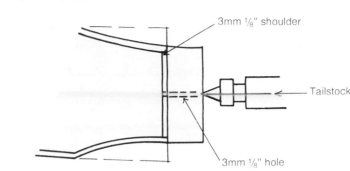

FIG 4 Diagram of plug

3mm ⅛" shoulder

Tailstock

3mm ⅛" hole

Now the design is starting, from the inside out. A template may be used if it seems difficult to make long tapers smoothly.

The flat bottom produced in drilling can be rounded out with the boring bar. This extra amount of weight gives the tall vase more stability.

Now take a 1200 RPM 6mm ¼" drill with an extension rod and a 50mm 2" sanding drum on the end. With the lathe running in the opposite direction as the drill, the sanding operation begins. A special bullnose end on one of the drums will clean up the round bottom. Work clear down through the abrasives to 400 wet or dry, keeping the dust cleared out with a vacuum frequently.

Some of the vases are finished inside just as well as the outside when the turning has a carved through wall.

Before taking off the steady rest, a plug is cut to fit the top of the vase (Photo 20). Fit this into the inside diameter about 5mm 3/16".

Photo 20 A plug is turned to fit snugly the interior diameter. The outside of the plug is turned for a wall thickness of 3mm ⅛".

A shoulder is then made that determines the wall thickness of the vase. Normally 3mm ⅛" is about right. Drill a hole of this diameter clear through the plug (FIG 4). This allows the point of the rotating tail centre to be perfectly aligned.

The outside profile can now be formed (Photos 21 and 22).

Photo 21 Working down the taper on the lower part of the vase.

Photo 22 Completed profile with 12mm ½" DIA bottom stem for a future pedestal.

This follows the design established on the inside work. You can now see the effectiveness of the glue-up mounting process, still holding the turning by a 12mm ½" x 25mm 1" stem.

A coat or two of clear lacquer sealer is applied after sanding down to 400 wet or dry

Photo 23 Clear lacquer seal coat is applied. Ready to transfer to a jig for finishing or carving.

(Photo 23). Yellow cedar sands very well, due to natural oils in the wood.

Proceeding to the finishing process, a jig has been made to secure the vase in a horizontal position, but allowing ease in rotation for evenness of coats of red lacquer (Photo 24).

Photo 24 The tall dry-flower vase is now mounted in a jig. Red lacquer coats are applied, sanding between each coat.

It is vital to allow overnight drying between each coat and to hand sand out all distortions and imperfections. It takes at least eight or 10 applications to achieve an even surface.

While patiently going through these steps, you may dream up a design for the outside surface. While experimenting with an air brush and ink an abstract cluster of weeds emerged in the example shown (Photo 25). Working with a hand pen brush ▶

'My preference is for a soft matt rather than a high gloss. Matt does not fingerprint and can stand all kinds of oil from handling.'

Photo 25 Air brush and ink applied design.

developed detail and a few swallows (Photo 26).

As happens frequently, there is a need for contrast. Not being able to find a white wood in my stockpile, I visited a sculptor friend who came up with a leftover piece of white alabaster, just the thing for a top ring and matching pedestal. It added more weight and therefore more stability, too (Photo 27).

Photo 26 Hand brush work on design.

Before gluing on the top ring and pedestal, a final coating is required. Two or three *clear coats* are for the protection of the detail and red lacquer.

My preference is a soft matt rather than a high gloss (Photos 27 and 28). Matt does not fingerprint and can stand all kinds of oil from handling.

The dope used by model aircraft builders does the job beautifully and has extra oil resistance and toughness. You can buy it from hobby suppliers.

I entitled my finished vase *Weeds and Swallows*. It was entered in an exhibition and received a second place ribbon for 3-D work.

Other examples of my work in yellow cedar can be seen in the other photos. ■

Photo 27 Finished dry flower vase with alabaster top ring and pedestal 3¼″ DIA x 16½″ high.

Lidded boxes with black lacquer lids, 180mm 7″ DIA x 115mm 4½″ H and 120mm 4¾″ DIA x 75mm 3″ H.

Classic vase, black lacquer, yellow cedar. Birdseye burl top ring, carved vines and berries.

Bamboo tall containers in British Columbian bamboo, with American black walnut lids 405mm 16″ H x 75mm 3″ DIA, and 355mm 14″ H x 95mm 3¾″ DIA.

A pair of vessels in yellow cedar birdseye burl, 115mm 4½″ DIA x 150mm 6″ H and 63mm 2½″ DIA x 75mm 3″ H.

Photo 28 Close-up showing detail and type of finish obtained.

Keith Rowley served his time as a turner and joiner before joining Nottingham City Police. He has been turning professionally since retiring early from the force (as Detective Superintendent) nine years ago. Keith's book *Woodturning: A Foundation Course* was published by the Guild of Master Craftsman Publications in 1990.

In the early 18th century the growth of trade with the Middle and Far East heralded the restructuring of the social classes in Britain. Up to then there had been only two classes, one consisting of the nobility, the 'landed gentry' and ecclesiastical authorities and the other, of serfs and workers of different kinds, usually in their employ.

Resulting from the impact of this overseas trading, there emerged various levels of 'middle class', in the main drawn from trade, commerce, industry and craftsmen. This prosperity led to the building of many quality homes and was influential in developing new social habits and modes of family living.

The demand for quality furniture increased and, as tea began to be established as a favourite beverage at social and family gatherings, smaller tables of all types became in vogue.

The three-tiered tea table or dumb waiter, the subject of this project, is representative of one style of table made in the Victorian era. It was obviously intended to serve a family or small social group as the three tiers could accommodate a teapot, milk and sugar containers and plates for sandwiches and cakes.

While traditional profiles have been retained in the turned pillars and the three trays, I have incorporated a more con-

Making a Three-tiered Tripod Table Dumb Waiter

PART 1

KEITH ROWLEY

PHOTOGRAPHS AND DRAWINGS BY GEOFF FORD

'Turners may well find this project (part 2 starts on page 26) a challenge and a pleasing change from making the ubiquitous bowl. But to achieve an attractive, quality piece, care, patience and precise jointing are called for. Good luck!'

temporary design for the legs. These, in addition to being profiled, have been tapered and inlaid with a boxwood stringing. Brass ball and claw feet have also been fitted.

The size of the largest tray (510mm 20″) has been influenced by the fact that many medium duty lathes are capable of swinging this diameter, either on the out-board end or by means of the swivelling headstock.

Many such tables were ornately carved with ball and claw feet, acanthus leaves, etc. Some, in fact, also had revolving trays, but these could well prove to be too great a temptation for mischievous children. It is not

difficult to envisage the sight of flying teacups and cucumber sandwiches!

Displaying Turnery

In addition to serving its original function, this attractive piece of occasional furniture can be put to alternative uses such as displaying selected pieces of china and cut glass.

For the woodturner, it affords a very practical and attractive means of displaying selected pieces of turnery.

The choice of timber for this project is important and

traditionally mahogany was used because of its dimensional stability, ease of working with hand tools and the fine finish it is capable of taking. The same species has been used in this project.

The photographs and drawings should provide all the information required to reproduce the table, although they should be carefully studied before the actual making starts.

Photograph 1 shows the finished project.

Photo 1 The finished table

Fig 1. Side elevation

Fig 2. Bottom of base pillar showing tapered slot dovetail and brass support plate

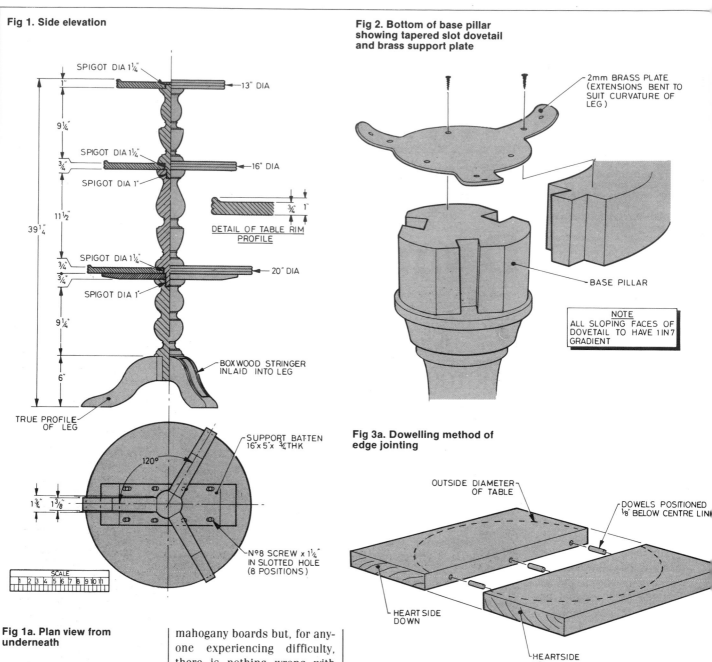

DETAIL OF TABLE RIM PROFILE

NOTE
ALL SLOPING FACES OF DOVETAIL TO HAVE 1 IN 7 GRADIENT

Fig 1a. Plan view from underneath

Fig 3a. Dowelling method of edge jointing

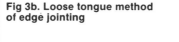

Fig 3b. Loose tongue method of edge jointing

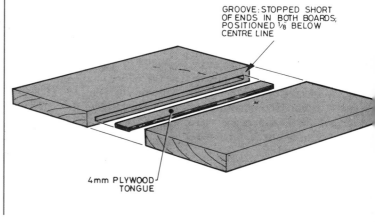

Fig 1 provides a side elevation of the project, and also shows the method of joining the pillars and trays, Fig 1a provides a plan view as seen from underneath.

Fig 2 shows an exploded view of the bottom of the base pillar, the tapered slot dovetail and support plate.

Order of Work

I commenced this project by making the three table tops or trays, which are 510mm 20″, 405mm 16″ and 330mm 13″ diameter respectively. It is still possible to obtain wide mahogany boards but, for anyone experiencing difficulty, there is nothing wrong with edge jointing two or more narrower boards to obtain the desired width. There are several ways of edge jointing and two methods are shown, i.e. by dowelling (Fig 3a) and the loose tongue system (Fig 3b). (Woodturners who possess a 'biscuit jointer' may well wish to make use of it for edge jointing. It is very quick and accurate.)

The boards to be edge jointed should be arranged to provide the best grain matching. To minimise the tendency of wider boards to 'dish', it is also advisable to alternate the annual rings, 'heartside up, heartside down' as shown in Fig 3a.

Making use of a try plane (or the longest plane you have), plane or 'shoot' the edges of the board and make sure that the mating edges are both dead flat and square. **The importance of achieving this cannot be over stressed because failure may result in a weak joint, and insufficient thickness of timber being left, by the time it has been turned true.**

The technique of using a try plane for 'shooting' edges is to ensure that downward pressure is applied to the front of the plane at the commencement of the cut but transferred to the rear end of the plane as the far end of the board is reached. (Fig 4). (Readers fortunate enough to own a planing machine should be able to produce perfectly matching edges in a matter of minutes.)

Check the accuracy of the mating edges by securing one board in the vice and placing the other on top. When satisfied that there is no light showing through the joint AND the boards are perfectly aligned (a straight edge held on the faces will determine), set out the position of the chosen edge joint.

For the dowels, carefully mark out the location with try square and marking gauge and drill the appropriate sized holes. These should be slightly countersunk to facilitate easy location and also to provide glue space.

In the case of the loose tongue joint, the grooves should be 'stopped' a couple of inches from each end. They would look unsightly when finished turned if taken to the ends. (To allow for the turning of the sunken tray tops without exposing the joints, the grooves and dowels should be positioned about 3mm ⅛″ off centre. (Figs 3a and 3b).

Cascamite

Apply the glue of your choice (I prefer Cascamite for this type of work) to the dowels/tongues and along the mating edges, then sash cramp them together and leave overnight. I normally

Fig 4. Technique of using try plane in edge 'shooting'

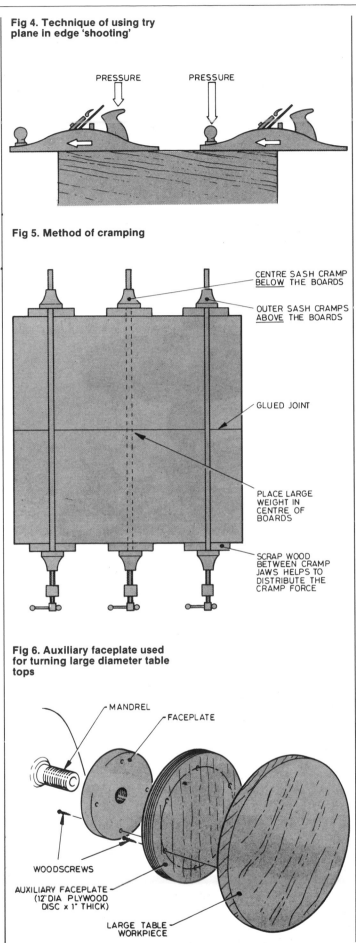

Fig 5. Method of cramping

CENTRE SASH CRAMP BELOW THE BOARDS

OUTER SASH CRAMPS ABOVE THE BOARDS

GLUED JOINT

PLACE LARGE WEIGHT IN CENTRE OF BOARDS

SCRAP WOOD BETWEEN CRAMP JAWS HELPS TO DISTRIBUTE THE CRAMP FORCE

Fig 6. Auxiliary faceplate used for turning large diameter table tops

MANDREL

FACEPLATE

WOODSCREWS

AUXILIARY FACEPLATE (12″DIA PLYWOOD DISC x 1″ THICK)

LARGE TABLE WORKPIECE

place a 56lb weight on the middle of the boards to keep them flat. (Fig 5.)

While these methods do not add substantially to the strength of edge joints, they certainly add to the ease of location and prevent the boards sliding about when cramping together.

When the glue has set, remove the cramps and clean up the undersides with a smoothing plane. Prepare all three trays for the lathe by bandsawing to slightly over finish diameter. If a large diameter faceplate is not available, a disc of 20mm ¾″ thick plywood, 305mm 12″ or 355mm 14″ in diameter, can be screwed to your largest faceplate to provide more support for the two larger trays when turning. Additionally, this auxiliary faceplate allows for the boring of the central holes without fouling the metal face plate with the drill bit. (Fig 6 and photo 2.)

Photo 2 Tray fixed to auxiliary faceplate

Make sure the lathe speed is adjusted to be compatible with these large diameters. Then, making use of a 10mm ⅜″ or 12mm ½″ bowl gouge, true up the face and edge until the required diameter and thickness are arrived at. Remember to use the gouge well over on its side and in the bevel rubbing mode.

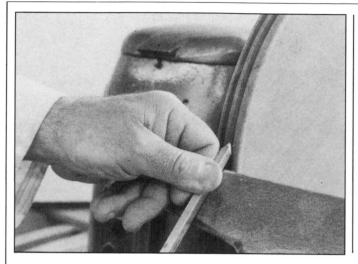

Photo 3 Forming beads on the tray edge with a skew

'Laws'

The peripheral speed, particularly on the largest tray, can be quite intimidating so it is vital that all the 'laws' of woodturning are observed or a gigantic 'catch' may ensue.

It is good practice to complete the beads on the tray edge and the inner moulded section before removing the bulk of the waste wood between these profiles and the centre of the tray. This way, maximum stability is retained.

All the beads and inner moulding can be fashioned with scrapers, which, if sharp, will leave a good finish. I personally use a 10mm ⅜″ spindle gouge and skew chisel, but beware, strict bevel rubbing is required! (Photo 3.)

Now remove the remainder of the wood to form the 'sunken' tray, either by pulling the gouge from centre to rim or by pushing from rim to centre. Make sure in both cases that as much bevel as possible is rubbing and use a straightedge at frequent intervals to check for flatness.

Any slight undulations can be levelled by making use of a square end scraper, **but be very careful when scraping near the edges of the two wider trays.** Any deflection of the wood away from the scraper will result in a catch and the

resultant damage will take some moving and probably leave the tray too thin in section. To prevent this deflection I place the fingers of my

Photo 4 Using the fingers in the supporting technique to prevent deflection

left hand behind the whirling disc and apply an equal and opposite force to that being applied to the scraper. (Photo 4.)

The through holes forming the joints on the two larger trays can be formed with a parting tool and skew chisel (used on edge and scraper fashion) or by the more accurate method of boring on the lathe with the appropriate size bit held in the Jacobs chuck secured in the tailstock. (Photo 5.) This however cannot be done on some types of lathes, e.g. swivelling headstocks.

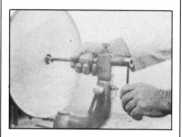

Photo 5 Boring the 32mm 1¼″ holes on the lathe

The blind hole on the underside of the top tray may have to be bored off the lathe, making use of brace and bit or pillar drill. A Forstner bit is most suitable for this because it has no screw point that would probably go through the top of the tray.

Photo 6 Power sanding the trays on the lathe

Finally sand the trays. To avoid unsightly circular scratches, I find it best to power sand, using 150, 220 and 320 grits in that order. Whatever method of sanding you use, be careful to avoid destroying the crispness of the moulded profiles. (Photo 6.) ■

NO EXSKEWSES NOW!

ALLAN BEECHAM

Allan shows how to cut beads with the skew without catching a crab.

Allan Beecham comes from generations of woodworkers and turners. He began on the lathe aged 13, learning his skills from his father and a number of firms in the East End of London.

He then worked in his family turning business until 12 years ago when he branched out on his own and set up Calamus Woodturning, first at Horam and then Burwash in East Sussex.

Allan and his work were featured in July/August, Issue 9 of *Woodturning*.

Photo 1 Start with the skew flat on its widest edge.

Photo 2 Start to move the tool round . . .

Photo 3 . . . until the skew finishes flat on its narrowest edge.

Robert Fritz once said: "Anything worth doing is worth getting wrong." Well, that may be true, but we don't want to go on getting it wrong for ever.

I want to deal with a technique that causes problems for many woodturners — how to use the skew chisel without 'catching a crab' as we called it in the East End of London.

I speak as a professional woodturner whose work is 85 per cent spindle, or between centres, turning.

This article on the skew is not going to be a treatise on the third party of the first part or the axial differentiation of the syncopated ninge wheel. Oh no — this is going to be as simple as me, and that's very simple I can assure you.

Angle or rake of skew. The rake or angle of skewness of the tool is most important. Try to get a rake of 70-75 DEG (FIG 1).

The reason this is important is that if you try to turn a bead with a rake of 55 DEG (FIG 2) you may find that even the slightest wobble when cutting the bead is likely to pull the tool in towards the bead and cause you to crab, or catch. With 70 DEG there is more control.

Bevel angle. This should be 25-30 DEG (FIG 3). This is the best bevel angle for sharpness, yet it is not too thin and weak so as to be liable to break out in hard woods like oak.

My father also used this angle, the only difference being that his tools were hollow ground, whereas mine are high speed steel (HSS) and flat ground.

After a one-day course with John Sainsbury I adopted his method of sharpening all gouges and chisels on a 100mm 4" wide linisher, or belt sander, with a 120 grit aluminium oxide belt.

This of course gives a flat ground bevel and, as John says, you have more bevel to rub and less chance of crabbing than with hollow ground tools.

John had a less steep bevel angle on his tools, about 40-45 DEG. There are problems with this angle. One is that I suspect the tool is not quite as sharp. The other has to do with the angle of presentation of the tool to the work, and I shall deal with that later.

Angle of tool on the rest. When cutting the left hand side of the bead, instead of holding the angle of the chisel to the right (FIG 4), try holding it with the angle slightly to the left, opposite to where you finish up (FIG 5 and Photo 1).

Of course you are rubbing the bevel on the top with the very edge of your chisel — what could be called the leading edge. The reason for this is that it facilitates easy access to the bottom of the bead where you have previously chopped in. It also eliminates

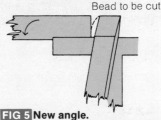

Tool rest.

FIG 4 Angle of tool on the rest. Old angle.

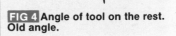

Bead to be cut.

FIG 5 New angle.

the need to move the tool along the rest, unless you are cutting a large bead or a half ball.

Another way to think about it is that when you are cutting down on the end of a piece of wood to get it clean, you use the edge of the chisel to rub at the same time as the long point is cutting. Now, turning this idea on its head and using the short point for cutting a bead, and utilising the concept of rubbing the leading edge, you can see that you will be using the same principle.

Returning to the short 45 DEG bevel angle of the skew, you will see that the other problem with this is that you would need to hold the tool further over to the left to get the leading edge rubbing, and consequently the fulcrum for the tool is further away.

A final point is that the chisel should start flat, with its widest edge on the tool rest, and it should finish with its narrowest edge flat on the rest.

In summary: 1) The point and leading edge both cut and rub at the same time.

2) Turn the tool over as you cut from the flat, sideways on, to upright.

3) Get both angles of your tool right. Now you have no exskewses for getting it wrong! ∎

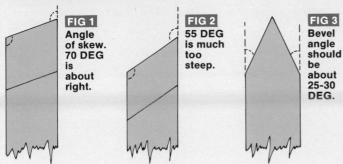

FIG 1 Angle of skew. 70 DEG is about right.

FIG 2 55 DEG is much too steep.

FIG 3 Bevel angle should be about 25-30 DEG.

Keith Rowley served his time as a turner and joiner before joining Nottingham City Police. He has been turning professionally since retiring early from the force (as Detective Superintendent) nine years ago. Keith's book *Woodturning: A Foundation Course* **was published by the Guild of Master Craftsman Publications in 1990.**

The next stage is to prepare the centre pillars and for these a piece of 100mm 4″ square by about 990mm 39″ long is required. A full size drawing and rod should be prepared to assist in the setting out (see Chapter 8 of my book, *Woodturning — A Foundation Course*). Even so, it may be considered advisable to first turn the pillars in some cheap soft wood to satisfy yourself that the profiles and proportions are to your liking. Much better than spoiling expensive hardwood.

The three pillars are best obtained from the same length of timber to ensure grain matching. Cut each pillar to the required length and turn all three to cylinders with the roughing out gouge. The next process is to bore the 25mm 1″ holes in the middle and base pillars that form the female part of the jointing method. This can easily be achieved on the lathe by means of the drill bit and Jacobs chuck held in the headstock. (I consider it good practice to complete any hole boring **before** the profiles are turned. This way, concentricity is maintained.)

It will of course be necessary to make a wooden plug to drive the two bored out pillars and this can be turned on a screw chuck, enabling the final shaping to be done.

It will be seen that the holes for the spigots in the pillars are

25mm 1″ diameter, but the holes in the trays are 32mm 1¼″ diameter. **Therefore** the male spigots must have the corresponding stepped diameters turned on them. (The reason is that joints in end grain seem to be slacker than in side grain. Accordingly, if the same size hole was used in the trays we would most likely have a tight fit in these, but too loose a fit in the pillars.)

Having completed the turning of the three pillars, dry assemble them and the trays. It is strange that when turnings are viewed off the lathe they very often look different. What you thought were nice flowing profiles do not look quite so pleasing in the vertical position. If adjustment to joints or profile is required, this is the time to make them. At this stage, it is also advisable to chisel in a couple of shallow grooves along the length of each spigot to allow surplus glue and air to escape in the subsequent gluing up process. Otherwise, the joints may spring open.

The top and middle trays should not require additional support, but the larger diameter bottom tray does. Prepare a batten as shown in Fig 1a and make the slotted holes to take No. 8 gauge woodscrews. This will be screwed to the underside of the lower tray and positioned **across** the length of the grain. This will check any tendency to warp and the slotted holes will allow for any shrinkage across the grain without the tray splitting.

Jointing

The jointing of the three legs or feet to the main pillar may be done in several ways. They can be dowelled or tenoned and these methods are satisfactory if care is taken. However, the traditional method, which is far from easy, is the tapered slot dovetail.

If this method is used, hand tools may be used or alternatively the bulk of the socket in the pillar can be routed out, making use of the routing jig/dividing head (described in detail in my book, page 130).

Making a Three-tiered Tripod Table Dumb Waiter

PART 2

KEITH ROWLEY

PHOTOGRAPHS AND DRAWINGS BY GEOFF FORD

In this final part of a project designed to stretch your skills, the author describes how to make the pillars and feet.

This method will result in three legs being positioned exactly at 120° intervals. Photo 7 shows the routing jig in use.

I used a 15mm $\frac{5}{8}$" flat bottomed cutter to remove the bulk of the waste and the resultant housing or slot, Fig 7a, provides a positive location for the template used to set out accurately the 'flats' on the base pillar. (These to receive the square shoulders to be cut on the feet.)

Fig 7b shows how the template is constructed. Component 'Y' should be a push fit in the routed housing and components 'X' should be equal in thickness and bevelled on their bottom edges to allow them to sit flush on the base pillar. (Obviously 'Y' + 'X' + 'X' should be equal to the thickness of the top of the legs.)

Fig 7b also shows the template

Photo 7 The router and jig in use to form the housings

located in the housing and component 'Z' fixed to enable the pitch of the dovetails to be scribed.

Fig 7c shows the final stage of setting out. The flats have been formed with a paring chisel and component 'W', screwed to component 'V', is used to scribe in the tapered slot.

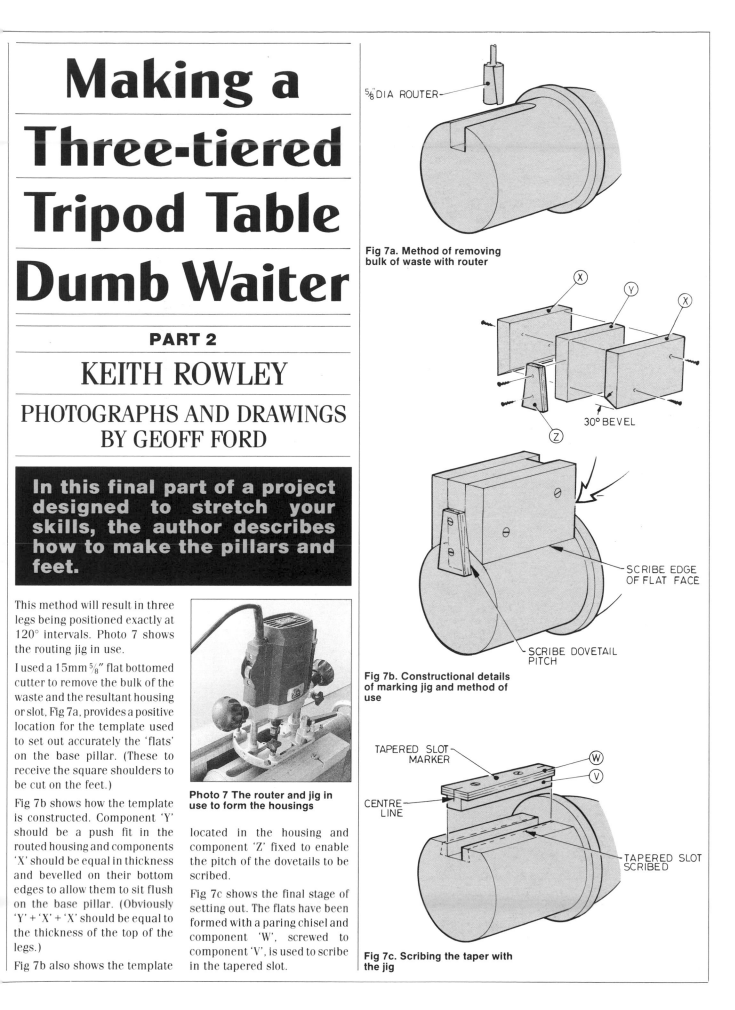

Fig 7a. Method of removing bulk of waste with router

Fig 7b. Constructional details of marking jig and method of use

Fig 7c. Scribing the taper with the jig

Photo 8 shows the flats being pared with a 32mm 1¼" bevel edge chisel and photo 9 shows the tapers being formed with the same tool. In both instances the wood is secured between the lathe centres, movement being prevented by engaging the dividing head.

Tapered Dovetail

The corresponding dovetails on the feet can now be prepared and again careful setting out and execution are required to form a good tight fit. Please note that components 'Z' and 'W' can be used to scribe the pitch and taper.

The great advantage of the tapered dovetail is that no cramps are required in the gluing up process and additionally the risk of splitting the central pillar is minimised as the joint only tightens on the last 6mm ¼".

The profiling of the legs should be left until the joints have been cut and tested. A cardboard or plywood template is made up and the outline pencilled onto the three legs.

For maximum strength, it is important that the grain is correctly aligned, avoiding short grain running across the width of the leg.

The bandsaw is used to shape and taper the legs, (45mm 1¾" to 35mm 1⅜") after which they can be cleaned up with files, scrapers and sandpaper. The grooves running along the length of the legs to take the boxwood inlay are worked with a scratch stock, a simple but very effective device which is easy to make.

A piece of a broken hacksaw blade, filed square and to the exact width of the inlay is inserted in the stock, positioned and secured by woodscrews. In use, it is 'scratched' back and forth until the required depth is reached in much the same manner that a marking gauge is used. Fig 8 gives constructional details of the scratch stock and Photo 10 shows it in use.

Photo 9 Paring the tapers on the sockets

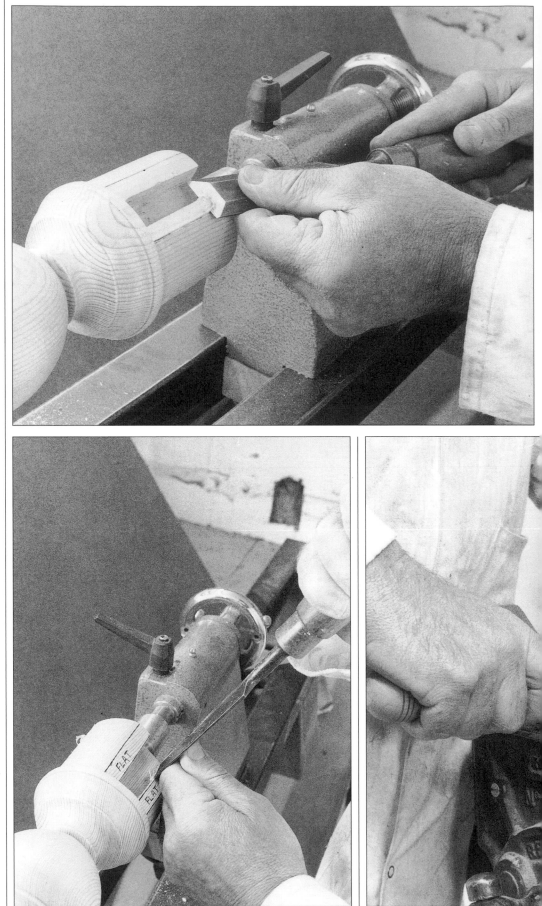

Photo 8 Paring the flats on the base pillar

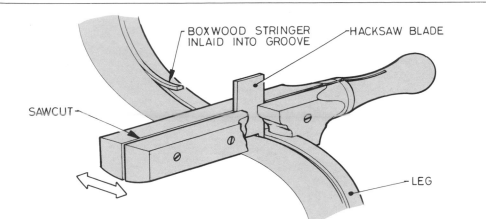

BOXWOOD STRINGER
INLAID INTO GROOVE

HACKSAW BLADE

SAWCUT

LEG

HACKSAW
BLADE
PROFILE

Fig 8. Using scratch stock to form grooves in legs for boxwood stringer

Photo 10 Photo-scratch stock in use

Inlay

The shorter grooves running at right angles cannot be cut with the scratch stock and are cut with sharp bevel edge chisels. The inlay should now be carefully cut to length and pushed into the grooves. The grooves should be slightly shallower than the thickness of the inlay, it being much easier to sand down the narrow inlay than the full width of the solid wood. If the inlay is a snug fit it can be sanded down (using a cork rubber and about 150 grit paper — along the grain) until it is flush with the leg.

Carefully remove the inlay and lay it out on a flat surface, sanded side uppermost and in such a manner that you can replace it from where it came. Now apply a couple of coats of sanding sealer and allow to dry.

Why go to all this trouble you might ask. The reason is, that mahogany will need staining to bring to uniformity of colour. When staining the legs it is extremely difficult to avoid the stain seeping onto the inlay so I stain the leg **before** I glue in the inlay. Obviously, very little glue must be used or it will be forced up the sides of the inlay and soil the stained area. Allow the glue to set and sand very lightly with some worn 400 grit paper. (If the brass ball and claw feet are to be used, the base of the legs must be profiled to fit them, before the staining process.)

Gluing

When all the component parts have been completed, 'dry' assemble the whole project to satisfy yourself that all the jointing is good. If you are happy, commence the gluing up process. I think it best to assemble from the base upwards, so glue the legs to the bottom pillar; the middle pillar through the bottom tray and into the bottom pillar; the top pillar through the centre tray and into the middle pillar; finally the top tray onto the top pillar. I then apply about 28lb of weight onto the top tray and allow the glue to set. If the joints are good I do not think there is any need to screw the trays to the pillars, but some may wish to do so. Obviously, the screw holes must be positioned so that they are cloaked by the pillars. **Remember to line up the grain**, particularly on the three trays, or the whole effect will be spoiled!

When the glue has set, the last constructional operation is to fit a metal strap of the type shown in Fig 2, which will add greatly to the stability of the joint between the feet and the bottom pillar.

Finish

Finally to the choice of finish and it does not really need me to remind you that this process can either make or mar the whole project. If mahogany is used, it will be necessary to stain to obtain uniformity of colour. On top of the stain

several options are available to us. (Remember to protect the already stained and inlaid feet from stain splashes. Simply cloak them in a plastic bag.)

French polishing always looks superb but, on a project of this nature, it is a job for the professional polisher, which means incurring a great deal of expense. This finish is also not as durable as some of the others.

Several brushed coats of thinned-down polyurethane, rubbed down with flour grade paper between each coat, provides an extremely durable and acceptable finish.

A sprayed finish is also worth consideration, having the advantage of being comparatively quick and consequently cheaper than French polishing. Most of my cabinet making projects are finished in this manner, but I have the advantage of having my own spray booth.

Finally, to the much underrated Danish Oil finish which will give a pleasing, satin finish that will not peel crack or chip. It is also heat and water resistant. It is absolutely vital that a good quality brush is used to apply the oil and I recommend squirrel hair brushes. Three or four coats are applied at 24 hour intervals, each coat, when dry, being lightly cut back with 0000 wire wool. A couple of coats of wax polish will also add to the lustre and enhance the finish.

Please note that it is sometimes more practical to stain and polish the component parts BEFORE gluing up, it being much easier to handle parts rather than the whole project. This, in fact, is what I did on this table, but of course even extra care is required in the gluing and assembly process.

Turners may well find this project a challenge and a pleasing change from making the ubiquitous bowl. But to achieve an attractive and quality piece, care, patience and precise jointing are called for. Good luck! ■

Peter Smith of Cincinnati, Ohio, has been turning part-time for several years now. He is a native of Aberdeen, Scotland.

Peter concentrates mainly on bowls of all shapes and sizes using the rich variety of native hardwoods found in the Midwest.

'Bowl fever' has burned up most of his spare time in the last few years. Two aspects of faceplate turning fascinate him — the technical expertise required in producing thin, uniform bowls, and the aesthetic aspect which is the balance of form, woodgrain, and weight.

The interplay of both of these factors he finds provides endless and ever rewarding challenges.

His main theme is to simplify, closing in on the classical forms for bowls and vessels which have evolved in many ages and cultures.

While turning is satisfying, giving rapid results, it is also an unforgiving craft.

Peter's rule of thumb is that if a piece, once off the lathe, needs explanation or reveals flaws that attract attention away from the basic design, then it is scrapped.

In between bowls and the demands of job and family, Peter finds time to turn out small turned objects such as tops, thimbles, boxes, pens, and letter openers.

KEEPING THE CORE

PETER SMITH

Wood pith is often thought of as something to avoid when turning. But Peter Smith argues that, provided care is taken, attractive vessels can be created with the pith still in the walls.

FIG 1 Traditional cut — 3 bowls

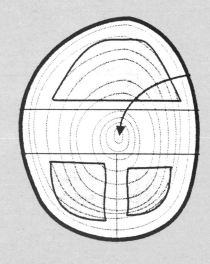

ıin-saw cuts

I t's against the rules, but hollow vessels can be turned with the pith as a major design element. The conventional wisdom is that the pith, or centre of a log should be avoided when turning, as pith is the most unstable part of the log and any changes introduced by drying out create concentrated stresses at the centre causing radial splitting.

In some timbers these splits grow wide and deep and can make a log useless for turning. In other woods, such as walnut, they are fairly superficial, extending into the wood about 12mm ½", and this can be sliced off to provide a fresh surface.

Traditional bowl shapes will distort badly and split with the pith, which is why, if you want to make a salad bowl, cut it out (FIG 1). To make use of the pith in a turned piece needs special design considerations.

Using the pith is not a new technique. I learned it at a workshop given by David Ellsworth. Indeed, the cover of the book *The Art of the Turned-Wood Bowls* by Edward

Jacobson (1985) shows a sphere by David with the pith clearly visible.

As Ellsworth said, "If I followed the rules, I would not be making these hollowed-out vessels in the first place."

To start, the wood must be freshly cut and green. If allowed to dry out, the log will inevitably split. The basic shape for these vessels is a thin-walled hollow sphere.

A sphere, by its nature, resists distortion as the wood dries. Thin walls are necessary, as any thickness will prevent the elastic deformation needed and create splits.

Even when these two needs are met, a small amount of splitting may occur, but these can be filled and will not usually detract from the design.

An advantage of this technique is that small logs of

even 125mm 5″ to 150mm 6″ DIA can be used. These would not make useful open vessels but can be turned into elegant hollow spheres.

I used wood from a limb a neighbour cut off an old apple tree to turn a series of bowls with the pith included and to explore styles.

Apple wood is particularly good because it distorts so much on drying. Indeed, the usual technique of rough turning a bowl, then letting it dry out for two to three months before final turning to shape, is often useless with apple because the blank will severely distort into an oval and by the time this is trued, little wood is left.

This characteristic of apple can be used to good effect if carefully balanced. Photo 1 shows a small-footed flat potato crisp bowl made from a crotch piece of the limb which has distorted nicely.

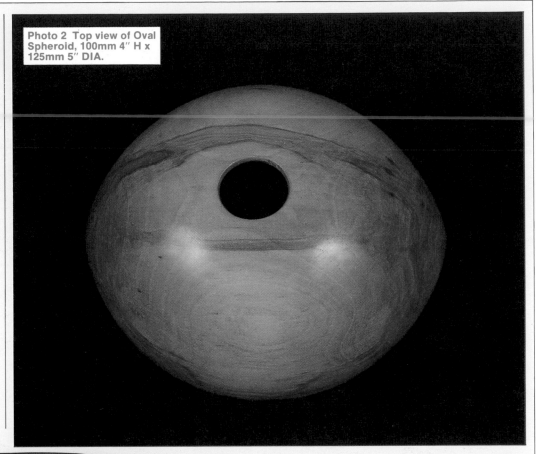

Photo 2 Top view of Oval Spheroid, 100mm 4″ H x 125mm 5″ DIA.

Photo 1 Potato crisp applewood bowl, turned wet, 190mm 7½″ DIA.

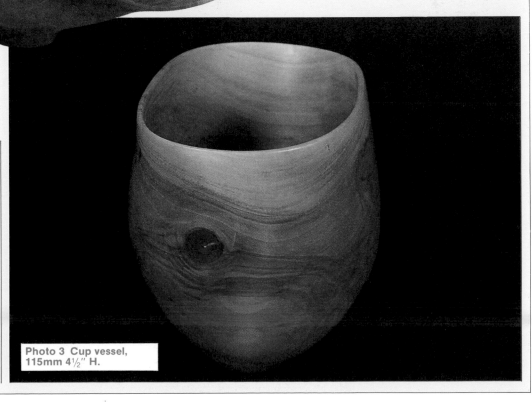

I started turning a series of hollow spheres as thin as I could through as small an opening as possible. Within a day of completion these vessels began to change shape and by the time they had stabilised two or three weeks later, had often distorted into rugby ball shapes (Photo 2).

Photo 3 shows a small cup-like vessel with a wide top. The distortion here is severe, turning the opening into an oval and bulging out the sides with the pith. This is interesting, but not elegant or finally acceptable. ▶

Photo 3 Cup vessel, 115mm 4½″ H.

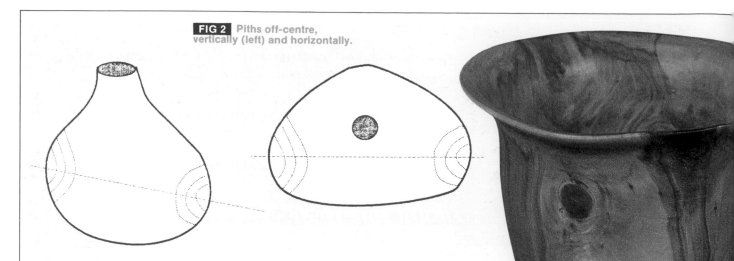

FIG 2 Piths off-centre, vertically (left) and horizontally.

Photos 4 and 5 show the results of careless positioning, also shown in FIG 2.

In Photo 4, one centre is not at the same height as the other and the vase leans to the side, while in Photo 5 the piths are not opposite each other through the centre, and the bowl has distorted into a triangular shape. Since all art is finally a question of balance, and the balance of these bowls is not good, they both join the reject pile.

Finally, Photo 6 shows a variation which is not recommended, namely turning the bowl directly with the grain (see also FIG 3).

Photo 4 Leaning vase, 125mm 5″ H.

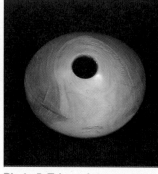

Photo 5 Triangular vase, top view, 75mm 3″ H x 100mm 4″ DIA.

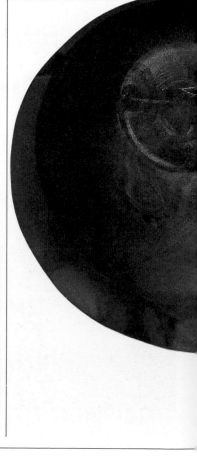

Photo 6 Bowl with centred pith, 140mm 5½″ H.

Photo 7 Base of bowl with centred pith.

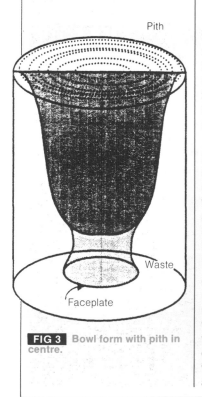

Pith

Waste

Faceplate

FIG 3 Bowl form with pith in centre.

Although distortion of the final vessel is relatively slight, making the bowl involves cutting into end-grain, which is unpleasant work and eventually the pith in the foot of the bowl has little flexibility to relax and splits are likely.

Photo 7 is a close-up of the base of the bowl. The pith is slightly off-centre and a large crack has developed. This was filled with the traditional glue and sawdust and is not serious. But on the whole, the problems here outweigh any advantages.

If the above variations demonstrate some of the ways not to turn these vessels, the results when all factors work well are rewarding — unique vases which distort symmetrically and show a balance which is aesthetically acceptable (Photo 8).

The process of working with pithy wood is as follows. Mount a log slightly longer than it is wide between centres, balance, then turn to a cylinder and rough turn down to a crude sphere (FIG 4).

Ensure the tailstock is constantly tightened, as the drive centre will slowly dig into the soft endgrain.

Remove the log and turn it 90 DEG, remount between centres and turn to a more complete sphere, making sure the pith centres are symmetrical and the marks of the drive centres are cut away.

Flatten one end to take the faceplate (or use waste wood glued on with cyanoacrylate glue for smaller pieces), remount and true up into a spheroid close to final form, leaving plenty of support at the

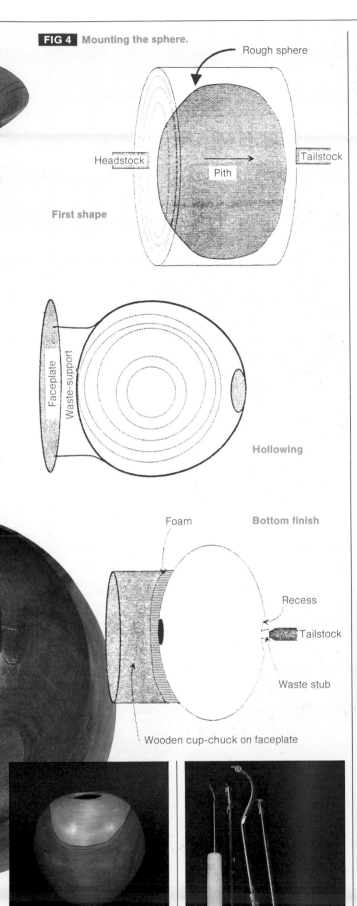

FIG 4 Mounting the sphere.

Rough sphere

Headstock

Pith

Tailstock

First shape

Faceplate

Waste-support

Hollowing

Foam

Bottom finish

Recess

Tailstock

Waste stub

Wooden cup-chuck on faceplate

Photo 8 Symmetrical vase, 150mm 6" H x 125mm 5" DIA.

Photo 9 Hollow-turning tools.

bottom for now.

Aim for flowing curves and balanced proportions. The surface should be approaching its final shape and smoothness, as once the bowl is hollow and thin, there is little opportunity, and much danger, in reworking the outside.

Begin the hollowing out with a small, about 25mm 1" DIA opening, and gouge vigorously with either the Ellsworth bent tool, the Stewart hooker, or the Thompson lance, depending on size and facility.

After every major cut, the lathe is stopped and the debris cleaned with a shop vac or blown out with compressed air.

The hollowing out is a slow process and must be done carefully to avoid deep grooves in the wall which will cause problems later. Take the whole sphere down to about 10mm $^3/_8$" wall cross-section.

At this time, finalise the shape of the bowl bottom, cutting away the bulk of the waste but still leaving 50-75mm 2-3" of support at the faceplate, and using the parting tool to define the bottom of the vessel.

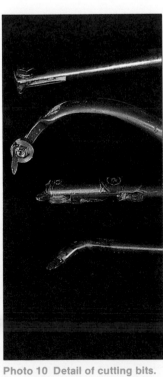

Photo 10 Detail of cutting bits.

Now the wall can be brought down to its final thickness of 6mm $^1/_4$" or less by very careful — and nerve-racking — cutting, measuring and scraping. Doubled-ended callipers, 180mm 7" and 255mm 10", are useful measures of wall thickness, or you can use the latest technique of a fibre-optic light inside the sphere to show the wall thickness.

There is no easy way to complete this stage. The general rule. is practice, practice, practice, and start at the top and work down the side carefully.

When final thickness is achieved, turn to the bottom of the bowl, finalise the lower hips and reduce the attachment to the waste block to a minimum (–25mm –1"). Now finish the surface, as described.

When parted from the waste, reverse the sphere into a cup chuck lined with foam, bringing up the tailstock to hold this in place and turn a small indentation in the bottom, then sand and finish.

Remove from the lathe, cut off the supporting cone with a small chisel, and hand finish.

Photos 9 and 10 show some of the tools used in hollow turning. Most use 5mm $^3/_{16}$" or 3mm $^1/_8$" square cobalt-steel toolbits.

For the simple homemade cutter designed by David Ellsworth, the neck of the square bit is ground round and super-glued into 5mm $^3/_{16}$" drill hole in a bent 10mm $^3/_8$" rod. This is versatile and useful for the top shoulder work but vibrates as it is extended into the bowl more than 50-75mm 2-3".

The Stewart hooker is well-known and deservedly popular, using both a 5mm $^3/_{16}$" bit, or the more aggressive 3mm $^1/_8$" cutter, which can be adjusted to various angles and, most usefully, replaced with a scraper blade to smooth out the grooves left by the cutter.

Jerry Glaser's swivel head boring bar is also shown, which ▶

works for depths up to 230mm 9″. A Jim Thompson lance is a much bigger affair but can provide delicate and clean cuts in larger bowls.

Each of these tools has its strengths and idiosyncrasies and all can be used in the process. Again, the only real secret to success is practice.

There are many ways to finish bowls. The method I have developed and used successfully can be applied to most turned objects, not just hollow spheres, and gives superior results.

Four basic steps are involved: 1 sealing, 2 power sanding; 3 oil hand sanding and 4 buffing. When the final shape has been reached and most tool marks removed by careful gouge work, use 100 grit paper to lightly sand the spinning surface.

Then the surface of the wood needs to be sealed with a lacquer-based sanding sealer which is liberally applied and then wiped off.

I use Deft Wood Finish, for two reasons. First it seals the wood and stiffens the grain, because sanding wet wood is ineffectual and the sealer sets the wood fibres. Second, as the wood darkens with the sealer, grooves and uneven surfaces stand out and suggest further tool work.

The bowl is then left to dry for 20-30 minutes, long enough for a lacquer-based thinner. This is often an awkward break in the flow of the work, but it can be constructively used for reflecting on the process — and making a cup of tea.

When the sealer is dry, it should be sanded, first by hand using 100 grit paper and then with a power sander, using Power-lock 100 grit 75mm 3″ discs, which give a smooth finish to the sealed wood. At this stage, tool marks and ridges can be sanded out and feathered in. After 100 grit, a 150 grit disc is useful.

When the surface is smooth

Photo 11 Cherry sphere, 255mm 10″, with only minor distortion and splitting.

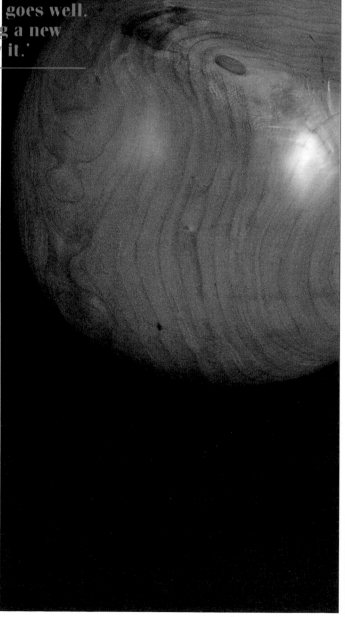

enough, an oil finish is applied and rubbed into the spinning bowl, using low revs (about 400 RPM) to stop the sandpaper skating over the surface.

The sequence is 150, 220, and 320 or 400 grit, with lots of Watco's Danish oil and hand rubbing. After final sanding is complete, the 'mud' wiped off and the surface relatively dry, the bowl can be parted from the lathe.

'The results are well worth the extra effort when all goes well. Woodturners seeking a new challenge should try it.'

The above sequence gives an attractive silky smooth matt finish which can be preserved by a few coats of artist's spray, Acrylic Matt. It can also be improved by a gloss buffing a week or two later, when the oil has totally dried.

Various buffing systems are available. The best I have found come from The Beall Tool Co. (541 Swans Road NE, Newark OH 43055, USA; tel: 614-345-5045) and uses three wheels: one made from linen, with Tripoli for rough shining, one with White Diamond finish to give a finer sheen, and a Carnuba wax wheel made from cotton which provides a high gloss durable wax finish. These three steps give a deep, lustrous surface to the wood, superior to any varnish or lacquer application.

So, as you can see, paying attention to the grain orientation, careful turning and hollowing, and giving a fine finish can create attractive vessels with wood pith still in the walls (Photo 11).

The results are worth the extra effort when all goes well. Woodturners seeking a new challenge should try it. ∎

Turning

Aviary

Abodes

ANDREW BARNUM

'Making birdhouses on the lathe has changed the way I think about woodturning and has expanded my appreciation of what a vessel can be.'

When I first made a few turned birdhouses in 1986 I had no idea that they would become something of a passion for me. I had every intention of forgetting about them and focusing on bowls and vessels as is the convention in contemporary turning. My thoughts however kept returning to birdhouses and the idea that they could be thought of as metaphors or symbols of man's caring about nature.

Birds themselves have been powerful symbols of freedom, harmony, beauty, and vulnerability for centuries. In religion, art, and literature the bird appears over and over in the form of a symbol. Isn't it possible, I thought, that the birdhouse could serve as a symbol of man's desire to preserve and maintain a place for the bird and those things for which it stood.

Thus began my exploration into Aviary Abodes. I've been at it ever since and am grateful for the luck I've had.

Lovers of folk art seem to enjoy the rustic models. One piece was made for a show at the Wustum Museum of Fine Art, and fine craft galleries have been receptive to other pieces.

I'd like to see a *Great American Birdhouse Challenge*, or even a *Great International Birdhouse Challenge* in the coming years. I believe that by combining creative craft with a concern for the environment, Fine Craft could be the most exciting and influential movement of the decade.

Aviary Abode in pine and cherry. The finished project

Andrew Law Barnum is a woodturner from Carmel, NY. In addition he is the co-founder and president of the Nutmeg Woodturners League, a local chapter of the American Association of Woodturners. He writes on the subject of woodturning. He also writes book and video reviews on woodturning.

I've been making decorative and functional birdhouses since 1986. I've used several construction techniques, but I like coopering because it is the most efficient way to use material. In conjunction with a stacked ring technique I use in the roofs, I

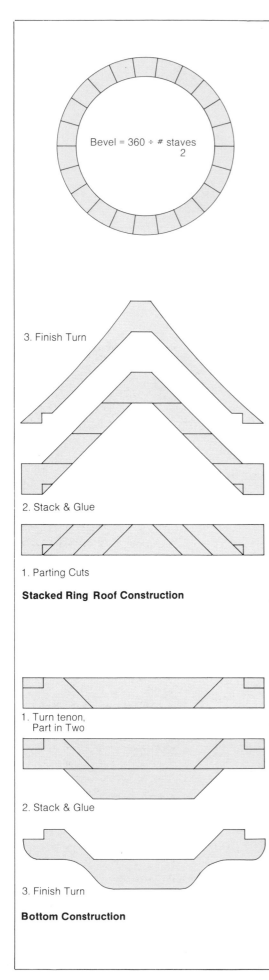

Bevel = 360 ÷ # staves
2

3. Finish Turn

2. Stack & Glue

1. Parting Cuts

Stacked Ring Roof Construction

1. Turn tenon,
Part in Two

2. Stack & Glue

3. Finish Turn

Bottom Construction

can build a three dimensional object from flat stock with practically no waste. This has become even more appealing lately because we're all becoming more aware of the importance of preserving our natural resources.

Body

The coopered birdhouses I make utilize a cylindrical body made from 22 bevelled staves. Twenty-two may seem like an arbitrary number but I like the proportions of the individual staves and the fact that it minimizes waste. As few as eight staves could be used, provided that the result is pleasing to your eye. Whatever number of staves you choose, use this formula to determine the bevel to saw on each piece: Bevel = 360 divided by $\frac{\text{\# staves}}{2}$.

At one time I would glue up the body into two half sections, then plane or joint out any imperfections in the mating halves. Now I prefer to take extra pains to tilt my saw to the exact bevel needed, thus eliminating one step in the process. Remember though that errors accumulate, so that $\frac{1}{4}°$ error adds up to 11° in a 22 stave construction. By cutting staves oversize and making a trial assembly, you will be able to make corrections if necessary.

I use common hose clamps to hold the staves together during glue-up, sometimes joining two together to gain extra length. Epoxy, Resorcinal resin and water resistant PVA have all provided good results for me. PVA, being a one part glue, is easiest to use.

When the glue has completely cured I mount the cylinder between two waste blocks; one screwed to the faceplate, the other pressed against the body of the live centre. I depend on friction to hold it all together, but double stick tape or cyano-acrilate would provide more security.

Start turning at a slow speed and true up the cylinder with a roughing gouge. Finish with the

Maquette for a Silent Spring, 1991. Native pear

Early Piece. Pine and fir, 1986

skew if you like, otherwise, use the gouge to produce a smooth cylinder. Sand smooth, starting with coarse paper, backed up with a felt or foam pad. Without skipping grits, continue down to around 220 grit paper. Functional birdhouses don't need to be turned on the inside, but it can be done by using a chuck like the one Jack Straka describes in 'Master Wood-turners' by Dale Nish.

The entry hole and perch hole can be drilled now, before you remove the body from the lathe.

Colour photos: Dennis and Iona Elliott

**Ode to Rachel Carson, 1991.
Burly myrtle**

**Silent Spring Variation, 1991.
Walnut and assorted woods**

**Wustum Variation, 1990.
Walnut, ebony and assorted
woods. Made for a show at
Wustum Museum of Fine Art**

**Portrait of Wren Cottage in
wormy ash, 1991**

**Manse in Pine, 1989. Pine,
assorted woods and gold leaf**

Manse in myrtle burl, 1991

I just use a hand held power
drill with a spade bit. The size of
the entry hole will be determined by the type of bird you
are trying to attract.

Roof

To turn the roof without wasting
material, I use a stacked ring
technique. Here's how it works.

Start by mounting a waste block
on the faceplate, and make it
the same diameter as the roof.
The waste block must be truly
flat, so if it does not run true
take a straight scraper and
remove any irregularities. Next,
bore a 20mm ¾″ hole through
the centre for later use. True up
your roof material and band
saw it into a disc, then press it
against the waste block with the
live centre. Use a divider to
mark off the rabbet ('rebate' for
UK readers) where the roof will
fit over the body, then mark off
the rings, usually about 15mm
⅝″ apart. If you can't picture
what the roof will look like, take
a piece of graph paper and put
it all on paper before doing any
turning. Sometimes I'll add
discs to the roof top to get a
trumpet shape.

I make my own parting tools
from .050″ or 3mm ¹⁄₁₆″ high
speed steel, but you can use the
narrowest parting tool you have
in your tool chest. Turn the

The roof, ready to turn

Turning the roof

The base, glued and clamped

Turning the finial

The body, glued and clamped

Clamped body and sawn staves

Clamped body with turned body

Black and white photos: Paul D'Agostino

Body, mounted and ready to turn

Parting the roof into rings

Set of rings with glued up roof

Roof rings with .050″ parting tool

Clamping with glued rings

Turning the roof

rabbet first, then hold the parting tool at around 45° and part through the disc. The angle of the cut will keep the loose ring from falling off, but it's best to remove each ring as you proceed to reduce the chance of

breakage. I use a snug fitting dowel with a brad centre to slip through the hollow headstock spindle and mark the centre of the roof for later use.

Once the roof is cut into rings, set aside the stack of parts and turn the waste block down to the size of the roof rabbet. Place the first ring on the waste block, apply glue and line up each ring in turn. Finally, glue the top piece which will be aligned by using the centre mark made earlier. The tail centre holds everything in place and acts as a clamp while the glue dries.

Once the glue has cured, the roof can be turned right on the waste block while holding it firmly with the live centre. Sometimes I'll turn courses of shingles, other times I go for smooth continuous curve. Bore the hole for the top finial while the roof is snug on the waste block by fitting the Jacobs chuck in the tailstock.

Bottom

The turning of the bottom is essentially the same as the roof. The bottom however will need a tenon which will fit inside the body. Make the fit loose so the body won't shrink tight around the bottom and crack. I like to use two or three brass screws or pins to hold the bottom to the body. The bottom should be removable for annual cleaning.

The finials and perch can be rough turned between centres, the tenons, of course, are turned exactly to size. Final turning is done with the tenon held in a Jacobs chuck mounted in the headstock.

Finish

When the parts have been turned, it's time to think about finishes. I like to apply the finish before final assembly, and I think that any exterior or marine finish will work well.

It's best to avoid getting any finish inside the piece, as the fumes will persist for a long time and discourage any prospective occupants.

Aviary Abode in pine and cherry (the finished project)

When the finish has dried, glue in the finials and perch. Use a flexible acrylic caulk between the roof and body to allow for wood movement. To fasten the bottom, drill three small holes through the body and into the tenon for removable pins. It's a good idea to drill a few inconspicuous drain holes so that water blown in will not be trapped.

Mounting

To mount the piece against a wall or tree, just drill a hole in line with the entry hole. At the same time drill through a spacer strip which will allow for the roof overhang.

Extensive research has been done on the subject of cavity sizes and entry holes as well as height and location of bird-houses. The best source of information on birdhouse dimensions for your region is in your local library. In the US, the Department of the Interior, Washington DC has a booklet entitled Homes for Birds, which contains lists of dimensions. In the UK, similar information can be obtained from the Royal Society for the Protection of Birds, The Lodge, Sandy, Beds SG19 2DL.

Making birdhouses on the lathe has changed the way I think about woodturning and has expanded my appreciation of what a vessel can be. I hope making turned birdhouses will provide you with the same pleasure. ∎

Door handle for sheep pen gate

Knobs and Handles

ERNIE CONOVER

Ernie describes how the science of latheology can help you make household chores more interesting and fun.

Ernie Conover is our contributing editor in America. He teaches woodworking in general, and woodturning in particular, at Conover Workshops, a school he and his wife Susan operate together. In addition to writing and lecturing widely, he is a technical consultant to a number of companies on design and manufacture of woodworking tools and machines.

I thought I might talk about some practical household applications for turning. That is, useful turnings. Things that will wow your friends and please your spouse to be sure, but practical none the less. I know it is incomprehensible to most turners that one could actually turn something practical but it is possible, **even easy!**

In fact the lathe is one of the most useful tools there is and opens new vistas of creativity. A lathe is so useful that I have vowed to give each of my children one as a wedding present when the time comes. In a future article I would like to point out a bevy of useful things that can be done with the lathe.

Paint Stirring

For instance, stirring paint. Simply turn a recess, the diameter of the paint tin you want to mix, in a piece of plywood mounted on a faceplate. Ease a live centre, and a corresponding recessed plywood ring, up against the lid to trap the entire can and turn the

lathe on at a low speed (300 rpm or lower). Leave it run for 15 or 20 minutes and you have thoroughly mixed paint, stain or varnish. If you are worried about flying finish, put the can in a plastic bag before mounting.

I naturally turn to the lathe to solve problems — what my father and I call the science of latheology. Hence, I incorporate turnings in most things I build or restore. I have put together a photo essay of these useful knobs, handles and the like for my article this month.

I save small scraps of figured wood for knobs and handles. It is often wood around a knot — wood unsuitable for other purposes. A bit of careful cutting, however, will yield a spectacular knob or handle blank. I also like exotics for knobs but use them less these days due to the rain forest concern. Basically, I am running out my existing stocks and only buy tropical timbers that are not endangered.

Bit Brace Handles

I have always wanted a short throw bit brace as they are much better for bench work than the usual 200mm 8″ to 255mm 10″ affair that one finds at hardware stores and flea markets. One is still made by Stanley of England — a beautiful little nickel-plated brace with a 150mm 6″ throw. I sent to Woodcraft Supply of Woburn MA for one just before our Summer workshops this year.

Upon receipt I was most pleased with the metal work of the brace but disappointed with the light plastic handles. The more I looked the more they vexed me. I could not bring myself to use it until I replaced them. Removal of the plastic was easy, it was just a matter of removing three screws for the knob and snapping back the white plastic ferrule on the handle. I decided to utilize the white plastic ferrules in the new wood handle as they would look like ivory but harm no elephant.

For many years a large chunk of Brazilian rose wood has acted as a book end in my office. It was given to me by a fishing friend from the National Geographics, Louis Marden. He obtained several billets in Brazil while on assignment for an article about hummingbirds in 1962. (For the article, see *The Man Who Talked to Hummingbirds*, January 1963.) I had finally found a suitable purpose for some of this rare wood.

After cutting off a slab of the precious rose wood with a thin kerf blade, I hand planed both sides flat. The plastic knob was traced onto a corner of the slab and band sawed out. After squaring off, the remaining part of the slab of rose wood was divided down the middle to form the two halves of the handle. Photo 1 shows the sawn blanks with the corresponding plastic parts.

Next the two halves were paper jointed together. For paper joints I have found hide glue to be best in conjunction with

1. Bit Brace with parts laid out on circular saw. The plastic handles we will be replacing are shown with the rose wood blanks

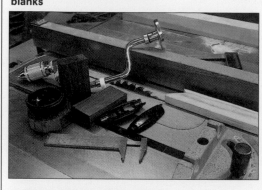

2. Gluing up of a split turning and the corresponding plastic handles we will be replacing

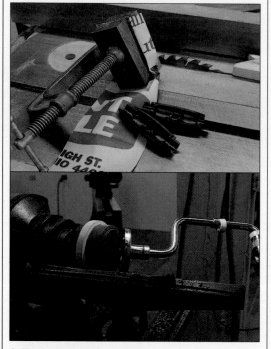

3. Knob blank hide glued to faceplate and ledge and recess for brace turned

4. Knob jam chucked and finished turned and French polished

brown craft paper. I use old grocery shopping bags which are perfect for the purpose. The hide glue should be rather

thick, the consistency of honey. Apply liberal amounts to both halves and mate them with the paper in between. It is necessary to work fast with hide glue as it will jell as it loses temperature. Clamp the two halves together in perfect juxtaposition and allow to dry for 24 hours. Clamping is very important both for good bonding of the glue and to have a thin paper joint. See Photo 2.

Knob

While the glue was drying I turned my attention to the knob. I hide glued this to a bit of wood mounted on a faceplate. I scraped a small depression in the wood so that a level ring was left as a glue area. This would hold the piece in question without forming an overly large glue area. Unlike the paper joint, this joint does not have to dry for more than an hour or so before turning. I used the tailstock as a clamp to hold the knob blank against the faceplate while the glue dried.

Using a 6mm ¼″ spindle gouge I rounded the billet and faced it. Next I turned the depression by cocking the gouge 45° to the left (the flute faces about 10:00 o'clock) and plunging it into the exact centre of the work. I swept the gouge left, using my thumb as a fulcrum, and ending up at the outer edge. Using the special box-making scraper that I sketched last issue, I scraped a recess to fit the brace as shown in Photo 3. The partially turned blank was now removed from the faceplate by breaking the glue joint with a large chisel.

The recess provided a perfect jam chucking opportunity. I scraped a pocket in a jam chuck that was the exact diameter and angle of the recess but also allowed the shoulder of the recess to seat on the face of the chuck. The handle blank was now running dead true. It was simple to now turn the profile of the handle with a 12mm ½″ spindle gouge, sand and French polish. The finished knob is shown in Photo 4.

5. Mounting paper jointed blank for handle on tapered mandrels

6. Paper jointed blank for handle mounted and ready for turning

7. The finished handle ready to split and mount on the bit brace crank

8. The finished bit brace. Much better than plastic and one that will really throw future archaeologists off!

I made the handle billet slightly oversize so that once the glue was dry the ends could be trimmed on the table saw, thus yielding perfectly square ends. After marking the centre a 12mm ½" hole was drilled exactly on the paper joint. Because a drill tends to wander with the grain, I drilled from both ends meeting somewhere in the middle. Something like the French/British tunnel under the Channel. The two holes only missed by ¹⁄₆₄".

Just to show that I do own a metal chuck, I used mine to

Once you get into the habit, the lathe will answer all kinds of problems. It is a friend you can turn to.

hold a bit of wood for the tapered mandrels. I turned both the plug and the mandrel with a shoulder that was the inside diameter of the plastic ferrules and which seated against the face of the handle. Photos 5 and 6 show the mounting operation.

Using the 12mm ½" spindle gouge the profile of the handle was turned effortlessly. The area to accept the ferrules was now scraped to the diameter of the shoulders of the mandrels. Finally a recess for the ferrule to snap into was turned with a very thin cutoff tool. Sanding and French polishing left the finished handle as in Photo 7.

To split a paper jointed turning, insert a large sharp chisel at one end of the joint and give it a light tap with a mallet. The piece should part into two exact halves. If it does not the glue was probably too wet and soaked through the paper. This

is why I prefer hide glue over white or yellow glue for the purpose.

I now used a carving burr in a shaft tool to carve a groove at the exact centre of the handle. This groove rides on a lump on the bit brace crank and keeps the handle centred. Once things fitted perfectly, I applied a heavy coat of cup grease to the crank and glued the two halves around it with hide glue. I applied glue to the tenons and snapped the ferrules in place and clamped everything in my bench shoulder vice. The grease prevented the glue from sticking to the crank and provides lubrication. After the glue dried, I filed the ferrules and glue lines flush and sanded everything smooth. A bit of French polish and I now had a world class bit brace shown in Photo 8, which served me faithfully through our Summer workshops.

Door Latch Handle

Another example of household use of turnings is a sheep pen door latch handle shown in Photos 9 and 10. It is simply

9. Door handle for sheep pen gate

turned from the same wood used throughout the sheep pen — poplar, a common wood in Ohio. I glued the handle with a new waterproof glue from Titebond. It looks and acts like normal yellow glue but is waterproof in all above waterline situations. I used an advanced sample sent to me but it should be on shelves by the time this article appears. It seems to work well and will answer many problems for architectural turners.

The latch is much better than the commercial variety because it can be opened and closed with an elbow while carrying feed, water and such. Likewise

it can be easily locked with a bit of twine.

Loo Handle

Sometime ago, in a fit of exuberance, our oldest child sheered the handle off of the loo. I was called from my lathe for urgent repairs. I junked the old porcelain knob, tapped out the 8-32 hole in the centre hub to 10-24, and turned a new

11. Flush handle for loo

ebony knob. The whole family was most pleased with the splendour of our loo as shown in Photo 11.

Door Bell Button

Likewise I installed an electric garage door opener. The button to open it from the house was of the early, plastic, Renaissance, tacky, awful variety. I was able to remove the switch from the plastic escutcheon. I then turned a new escutcheon from walnut and glued the switch into it. The finished work can be seen in Photo 12. I held the switch to the wall with double sided tape.

12. Door bell button

In closing let me say that most any household job can be made a lot more interesting with a bit of turning. Not only will the family be pleased with the results, the job will be a lot more fun with some turning. Once you get into the habit the lathe will answer all kinds of problems. It is a friend you can turn to. ∎

Dave Regester has been turning professionally since 1974. In his workshop at Tiverton in Devon he makes salad bowls, scoops and platters which he sells through high-quality kitchenware shops.

He also makes one-off artistic pieces which he sells through galleries and exhibitions.

O ne of the benefits of carrying out my trade in the same locality for as long as I have is that the word gets around that you like ugly lumps of wood that normal wood-workers turn their noses up at. That is why when one woman arrived at a local sawmill with an unsightly piece of burr lime they pointed her in my direction.

The sawmill was probably glad to get out of the job of dealing with this dendritic carbuncle (Photo 1) but I liked what I saw, although I was not inclined to make it into a solitaire board as suggested by the owner, who was fortunately persuaded by my careful explanation of the nature of burrs that this outgrowth cried out for conversion into a bowl.

All she wanted was a memento of a much-loved, now dear-departed tree which had been part of a locally well-known avenue leading to a stately home.

The problem with dealing with this sort of raw material is being able to envisage what it will look like when you have finished while not allowing too much wishful thinking to cloud your vision so you do not see the faults that may conspire to

Natural Top Bowls – The Burr Facts

DAVE REGESTER

How to turn an ugly dendritic carbuncle into an object of beauty — Part 1.

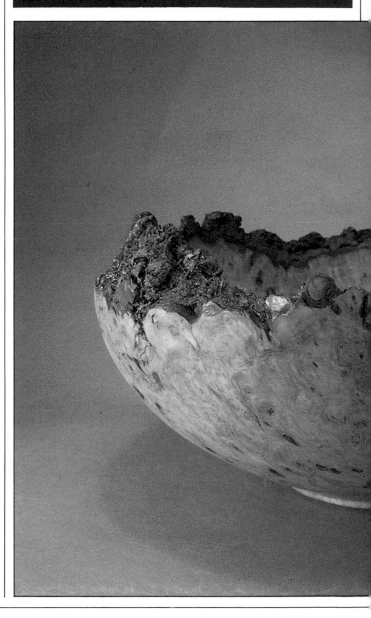

**Photo 1
The original burr lime dendritic carbuncle.**

make the wood unsuitable for your purpose.

In other words you need to keep your options open as you get into the lump so you can modify your plans if necessary. In this case the wood did exactly as I expected which I presume means that it was cut into shape by someone who either knew what they were doing or who were just lucky.

You can get some idea of the size of the burr from the photograph. Its exact measurements were 660mm 26" long x 510mm 20" wide x 410mm 16¼" deep. Its main faults from a bowl turner's point of view were that it was not round and it had a chainsaw cut in one end that coincided

Photo 2
A chainsaw cut coincided with a bark intrusion.

with a bark intrusion (Photo 2).

You can turn a natural-top bowl with a wildly asymmetrical rim but I have always found them less pleasing than those with a rim which is a closer approximation to level. This is because when you are turning the outside shape you are looking at the average profile — the top merges in a blur. The profile which looks good where the rim is one height does not necessarily look good where the rim dips.

A good way of working out where to make the rim so you achieve a good shape is to find a bowl in your collection of roughed-out bowls awaiting conversion that is roughly the right size and place the burr on top (Photo 3). As you can see this burr was quite uniformly rounded and looked promising for a fairly level top.

The bowl blank provided me with a means of supporting the

Photo 3
Judging how to shape the burr is aided by placing it on a bowl of similar size.

burr so that I could flatten the sharp ridge where the base of the bowl would be with my power planer (Photo 4). If you do not flatten the base you have no way of supporting the burr when you bandsaw it and subsequently mount it on the lathe.

The problem about preserving the bark top is that it is difficult to mark where to cut it. I usually do this roughly with callipers and wax crayon and rely on eye to get it right, but these ▶

Photo 4
Flattening the base of the burr with a power planer.

Photo 5
Marking the top of the bowl with end-grain sealer.

methods sometimes leave marks that I do not notice until I have finished and then they are difficult to remove. In any case I needed a method that would show up on the photo and I hit on a wheeze that may revolutionise life as we know it — but probably will not.

I found a part-turned, but fairly round bowl that was just the size I estimated the burr bowl would be and put it on top of the burr in the right position. I then painted round it with end-grain sealer (Photo 5) which I knew to be white when wet and transparent when dry, secure in the knowledge that even if it showed shiny after I had finished the bowl I would be able to buff it with a brush held in the drill and it would just produce a nice matt finish.

The sealer does not appear to show up particularly well in the photo because of the lichen also present that appears to be the same colour, but I assure you the sealer was quite distinct in real life.

I turn the outside of bowls like this between centres because this gives more support than a faceplate and allows some adjustment before you are committed to the exact position of the top relative to the sides.

It also means you do not have to make the base perfectly flat before you start to turn, nor do you need to be too careful about cutting the outside perfectly round. I cut it roughly to size on the bandsaw (Photo 6) but you

Photo 6
The blank roughly bandsawn to size.

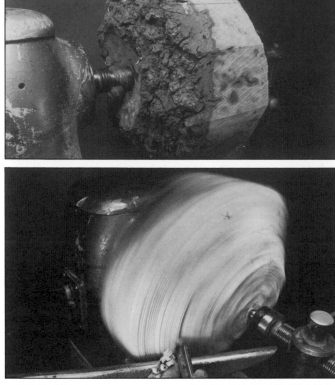

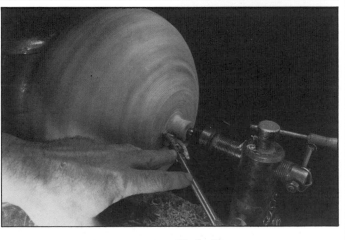

Photo 10
Hollowing out the recess with a 6mm ¼″ bowl gouge.

Photo 7
A flat is made on top of the blank for the driving centre

could do it with a chainsaw, provided you can adequately secure it.

The driving centre needs to have a solid surface to grip on so it is necessary to get rid of the bark in the centre of what will be the top before mounting the blank. I used an Arbortec blade in my angle grinder but you can use a carving gouge or chisel if you are not as mechanised as me. If you make a large flat area on top it will give you more options as to the eventual position of the blank (Photo 7).

Now the blank can be offered up between the centres and the tailstock adjusted to the correct distance from the headstock. Before you wind the dead or rotating centre up tight you can

Photo 8
Truing up the outside with a 13mm ½″ gouge.

rotate the blank and see whether you have it in the most advantageous position. It may be that you can see a way of exploiting a particular feature in the wood if you change the angle slightly or maybe you need to move it to avoid a void or defect.

When I have decided on the position the centres will be I

Photo 9
Marking the size of the base recess with callipers.

like to remove the blank and mark the position of the driving dogs by holding a spare driving centre in position and belting it with a mallet.

Before I start the lathe on a job like this I like to make sure it is set on the slowest speed and I always rotate it by hand to make sure there is nothing touching the blank. I usually start the lathe with no rest in place and stand well back out of the line of fire just to ensure that it is not so out of true that it will vibrate too much to turn.

This one was quite well-mannered but if it had proved

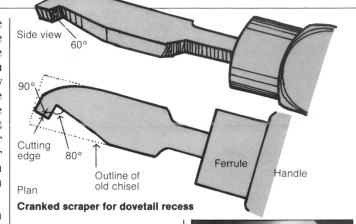

Cranked scraper for dovetail recess

unruly I would have got rid of any protuberances with the Arbortec. If you need to use hand tools for this you will need to remove the blank from the lathe to make sure you do not push it out of centre. I found this particular blank rotated without too much vibration at 250 RPM.

When the work is running true you are at last in a position to do some turning **but do be careful when positioning the rest because this sort of blank is the one most likely to have a bit sticking out to catch anything. I also recommend you wear some form of face protection, because with burrs the bits that come off are inclined to fly in all directions. I always wear an Airstream helmet.**

opportunity of checking the moisture content of the inside of the wood with a moisture meter, if you have one. If you have not got one and are in any doubt about the dryness of the wood I suggest you turn the bowl with nice thick sides, just in case it distorts too much or develops too many cracks after you have finished, so you can remount the bowl and re-turn it.

I rather like the way the grain in slightly unseasoned wood distorts after finishing so that you get a tactile suggestion of the appearance of the grain. I do not finish the outside of the bowl at this stage because I like to have the option of changing the shape after I have hollowed it out. I also do not immediately put the bowl into a centrally

'I hit on a wheeze that may revolutionise life as we know it — but probably will not.'

I use a ground back 13mm ½″ high speed steel bowl gouge for truing up the outside, but whatever you use it is no good expecting to take off a lot of wood quickly until the outside is true. So little by little is the way and remember to aim for the outside of that blur.

The gouge should be held on its side so that the hollow is pointing in the direction of cut, and you should cut from base to top so that if there is any normal grain the fibres you are cutting are supported by the fibres underneath (Photo 8).

By cutting this way rather than truing the side first the gouge bevel is supported by solid wood as soon as possible. You are also pushing the work onto the driving centre rather than away from it, and you are not standing in the line of fire if the blank should decide to go into orbit. You should tighten up the tailstock at regular intervals because the driving centre will tend to bore into the blank.

During the course of shaping the outside you have the

heated room.

When the outside of the blank is the shape I want, I turn the base by cutting from the outside in towards the centre using the same gouge with the hollow pointing towards the centre.

I like to re-mount this size of bowl, when I hollow out the inside, on the expanding dovetail jaws of the Axminster four jaw chuck rather than an ordinary expanding chuck because they are stronger and allow you to exert more pressure. But because of this extra pressure I like to make a deeper recess than I would for an ordinary bowl.

In any case I remove the recess on this type of bowl after I have finished the main bit of turning because I do not like the hard shoulders of the recess to interfere with the natural flow of the shape.

In this case I made the recess about 63mm 2½″ DIA x 6mm ¼″ deep. I marked it out with callipers (Photo 9) making sure that I touched only one point on

the base because if you let both points touch you get a catch.

I hollowed the recess using a 6mm ¼″ ground back HSS bowl turning gouge (Photo 10) making sure I went very carefully so the spigot supporting the blank at the tailstock did not get too thin.

As you can see from the photos the tailstock prevents you from making the dovetail sides of the recess with an ordinary straight scraper so I have ground a right angled cove into the side of an old chisel to make it into a cranked scraper with its cutting edge at such an angle that it forms the dovetail sides (see drawing).

I use it with the rest higher than the centre and with the edge pointing down (Photo 11) but it is very prone to catching because I am not used to holding a tool at that angle and there is not the whole of the tool in direct line with the cutting edge as in a normal scraper to give that extra stability.

At this point I turned off as much of the spigot as I thought I could so I had less to remove

Photo 11
Forming the dovetail side of the recess with a cranked scraper.

when I took the blank off the lathe (Photo 12). If you use the Craft Supplies combination chuck you will see it has a larger hole in the centre than the Axminster chuck. This means that if you use the combination chuck you do not have to remove so much of the spigot at this stage. The blank is then ready to be mounted on the chuck.

In Part 2 of this article I shall deal with hollowing out and removing the recess. ■

Photo 12
The spigot is reduced in size as much as possible.

Natural Top Bowls - The Burr Facts

Part 2

DAVE REGESTER

Dave Regester has been turning professionally since 1974. In his workshop at Tiverton in Devon he makes salad bowls, scoops and platters which he sells through high-quality kitchenware shops.

He also makes one-off artistic pieces which he sells through galleries and exhibitions.

In this final part of his article Dave describes how to hollow out the bowl and finish the outside.

In part one of this pair of articles on making a burr lime bowl I described how to convert the lump of burr to a bowl-shaped blank with a recess in the base to accept an expanding chuck. I began by holding the lump between centres and finished likewise.

The chuck used to hold the bowl for hollowing is the Axminster four-jaw chuck 127mm 5" DIA with dovetail jaws. Photo 1 shows a combination wrench with a universal joint being used to expand the jaws because this allows easier access at the back of the bowl and speeds up expansion. Before finally tightening the jaws I spin the blank by hand to make sure it is centred.

Hollowing out the bowl is dangerous because there are bits sticking out that are easy to forget when they are rotating and can catch your fingers. The irregularities also make it awkward to start the cut with the gouge because you cannot

Photo 1
Tightening the jaws of the chuck.

Photo 2
Removing the inside with a 13mm ½" gouge.

Photo 3
Finishing inside cut with a 6mm ¼" HSS gouge.

rub the bevel before you start to cut.

It is more important to rotate the blank by hand to check that it can turn freely before you start the lathe when doing this sort of bowl than with any other. Even if you are in the habit of adjusting the rest while a normal bowl is rotating, I strongly suggest that you stop the lathe to do it when turning natural top bowls.

Another job before turning a bark-topped bowl is to check the bark for bits of stone and dried mud which, if not removed, will blunt your tool edges. The first time you start to hollow out this type of bowl you will either be excited or scared depending on your attitude, but you will be more relaxed if you are wearing some face protection.

I always start hollowing with a 13mm ½" gouge with ground back sides (Photo 2) rather than the standard straight ground gouge because it allows a finer cut, and you must not try to take out much timber at this stage. If you push too hard early on in the process you will find the bark gathers around the edge and prevents it cutting cleanly.

I can start with the gouge because I know from experience the correct angle to hold the tool. If you are in any doubt you will be unable to rub the bevel to establish the angle because of the roughness of the surface, so I suggest you use a straight scraper to make a groove where the wall will be to give your gouge something to lean on.

Once you have removed the bark from the top of the bowl the hollowing out process is much the same as in any other bowl except you have to be extra careful about avoiding the irregularities of the top catching your fingers, the tool rest or the tool rest column.

If you are in the habit of touching an ordinary bowl while it is rotating to feel how smooth it is, or assessing the thickness of the walls, I suggest you consciously switch to a different, ▶

'Switch to a more cautious mental mode or keep a plastic bag nearby for the odd finger that will be removed.'

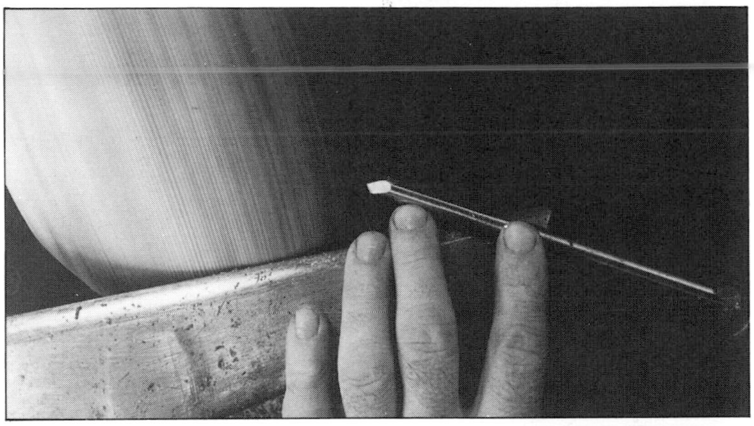

Photo 4
Finishing outside cut with the 6mm ¼" gouge.

Photo 5
Power sanding the outside.

Photo 6
Power sanding the inside.

Photo 7
The bowl supported between centres.

more cautious, mental mode or keep a plastic bag nearby for the odd finger that will be removed.

I find it quite difficult to assess the depth of a bowl as hollowing proceeds because of the irregularities of the top, but I can see the top of the bowl while it is rotating and roughly measure the depth from this by holding a ruler against the side. It is not quite so vital to make the thickness of the base exactly the same as the wall in a

fibres easier to cut.

This improved matters a bit but I could see that I could carry on fiddling all day and not improve the finish. I even tried a round nosed scraper but it tore the fibres so badly I had to revert to the 6mm gouge just to get back to the finish I had achieved before.

I soon realised the only way I was going to get a good finish was with power sanding, but before doing this I turned my attention to the outside of the

'This is the best moment in turning for me, when I see my efforts have turned an ugly lump into an object of beauty.'

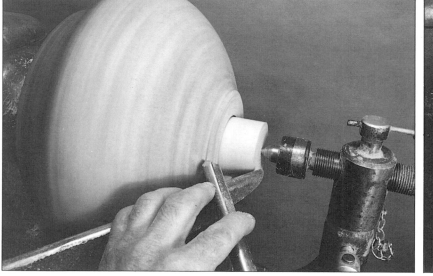

Photo 8
Finishing the bottom with the 13mm gouge.

Photo 9
The partly turned-away support.

bowl of this type as they should be quite chunky to match the roughness of the bark.

With this bowl I took out the middle until I reached the depth intended, and when I inspected the finish it was really rough. I was certain I could do better from the tool, so I then used a 6mm ¼″ high speed steel bowl turning gouge to take out some fine cuts (Photo 3).

By this time I realised that this bit of burr lime was not as dense as any other burr I had turned, and I found that however carefully I cut and however sharp the tool I could not get a very good finish — there were always some loose fibres sticking up. So I moved to plan B and sprayed the wood with some water which usually makes the

bowl which I attacked with the 6mm gouge (Photo 4) with the hollow pointing up and using the side of the gouge nearest the bowl to take off thin shavings.

This cut is definitely not for those of a nervous disposition for you have to start with the tool at the very edge of the top which is just a blur at this point. You have to know exactly the angle at which to hold the tool, for if you don't you will surely get a catch.

I left a small foot on the base (Photos 5 and 7). This will be removed after the bowl has had time to settle down and its removal will get rid of any warpage and the recess in the base.

I was able to do the whole of the outside in one smooth

movement which enabled me to make a good job of getting a smooth shape even if the wood was unwilling to produce a smooth finish. I used water to help with the rough grain and soon decided that the power sander would be needed on the outside as well as the inside.

I use 150mm 6″ disc pads for the outside of bowls (Photo 5) and 3M Stikit self-adhesive discs. I attach these with an extra layer of special adhesive which remains permanently sticky because all the dust generated soon dislodges the discs if you rely on the disc adhesive alone. I change pads rather than discs as I work through the grades from 80 grit to 100 and then 150 because the discs do not remain adhesive if you constantly remove them.

With a bit of practice the pads can be removed and replaced by a flick of the wrist rather than using the chuck key, but I cannot adequately describe this in words or photos. If it were not for the fact that some time ago I invested in hundreds of these pads I would by now be using velcro-backed pads of a similar size on the outside of bowls.

I use 50mm 2″ discs for the inside of the bowl because they fit easily into the tighter curves (Photo 6). I do not use these for the outside because they do not reach the base of the bowl before the headstock gets in the way of the drill.

This bowl had such fluffy grain I needed to sand in some places with the bowl stationary, which was no problem except it

**Photo 10
A clean bottom!**

was so soft I had to be extra careful not to remove too much in one place so it resulted in a hollow that would be noticeable after further sanding with the bowl rotating. I used 60, 120 and then 180 grit on the inside and followed up with hand-held 220 grit aluminium oxide cloth-backed abrasive.

I often use Danish oil for this type of bowl and in this instance it really brought out the colour well. The wood had looked disappointingly dull until this point and I got a real lift when this honey colour appeared. The bark also darkened which produced a nice contrast. This is the best moment in turning for me, when I see my efforts have turned an ugly lump into an object I find beautiful.

At this stage I put the bowl in a cupboard to settle down and after a day or two moved it into the house where it progressed

through the rooms from coldest to warmest so it gradually became acclimatised to the humidity. After several weeks of house training I decided it was sufficiently well adjusted to be allowed to go into the outside world and proceeded to clean its bottom.

In the case of a flat-topped bowl I normally do this by holding it in the wood jaws of the Axminster four-jaw, as described in my earlier articles Simply Good for Salads (pages 75 to 82). This does not work for a natural-topped bowl because of the irregularities of the top. It was for this same reason I thought it tempting providence to rely on an interference fit on a turned blank alone.

I therefore decided to support the top with a blank turned to the diameter of the inside of the bowl and held on a single screw

chuck. I supported the base between centres by sticking a short cylinder of scrap wood into the recess with hot glue and pressing the rotating centre into this (Photo 7).

I was then able to turn the bottom flat with a 13mm ½" gouge (Photo 8) until I had removed the foot and could see the floor of the recess. I did a smoothing cut with a 6mm ¼" gouge making sure the base was concave and then reduced the diameter of the supporting cylinder gradually so I did not place too much stress on the joint.

At the stage of Photo 9 I sanded the bottom so that if the cylinder parted company with the base I would not have much hand sanding to do.

After I had sanded the base I found I could turn more of the cylinder away and eventually found the bowl was supported

by the blank it was pressed onto with no assistance from the tailstock. Hence I was able to finish the bottom completely while still on the lathe so it was smooth enough to satisfy even the most critical of Australians! (Photo 10).

The special adhesive for sticking on the sanding discs is Bodyline disc pad adhesive, available from car body repair shops, or contact Bodyline Products, Great Eastern House, Greenbridge Road, Swindon, Wiltshire SN3 3LB. ∎

Creating
HARMONY
GEOFF HEATH

When the conductor of a choral society found her music stand in a state of collapse, Geoff Heath, a tenor as well as a turner, volunteered to make her a new one. Here he describes how to set about it.

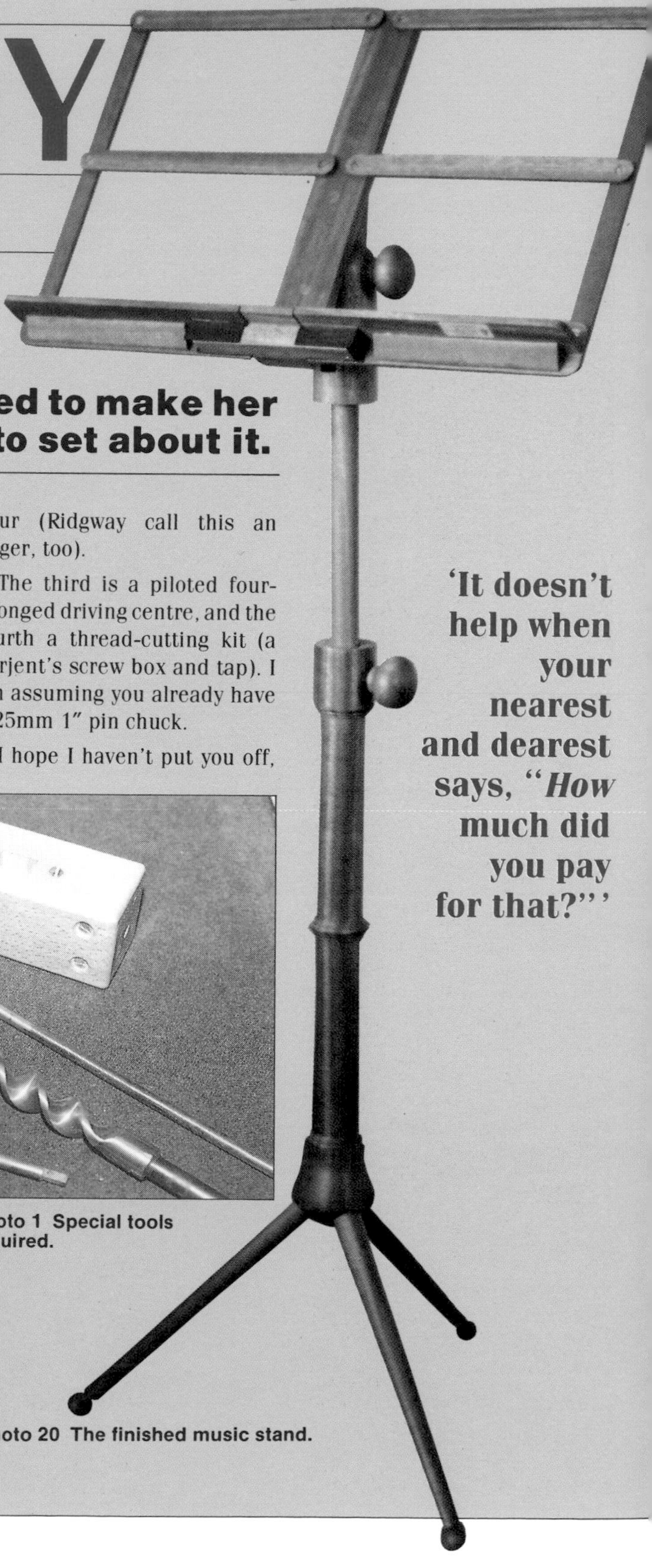

The memory of an old music stand I had repaired for a friend, made from a number of turned parts, remained with me and helped me build my new one. But I cut out some of its less practical features.

In essence, my music stand is a hollow, vertical tube (or 'spine') supported on tripod legs with a music desk on top.

The height of the desk can be adjusted by moving a slide within the spine, and its angle can also be varied. The legs can be quickly removed and the desk folded, making it easy to store or transport.

To make it I chose red meranti, as I already had the wood in suitable sizes. This is easily worked, but the grain tends to rough up unless shallow cuts are made.

Sometimes a project will force me to buy a special tool, which is used once and then discarded for ages in a drawer or the tool rack, making me wonder if I was wise to buy it.

You may have had the same experience. And it doesn't help when your nearest and dearest says, "*How* much did you pay for that?"

But then you do another job which demands that very tool and all the expense seems justified. Life is so much simpler when the right equipment is to hand.

This project calls for at least four special tools (Photo 1). And

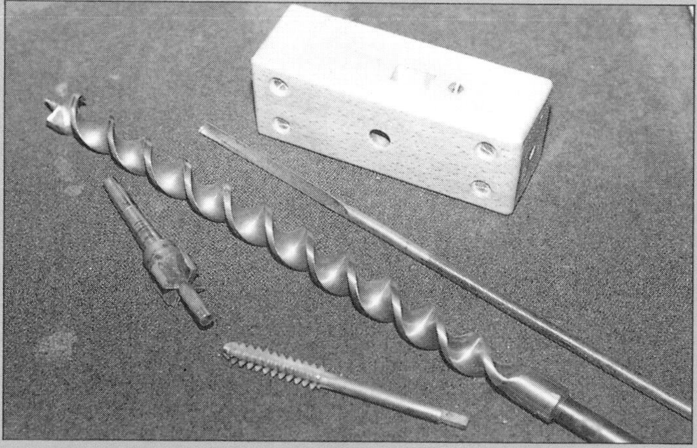

Photo 1 Special tools required.

if you haven't got them already you may need to convince yourself that you need them now.

The first is an 8mm $\frac{5}{16}''$ auger, which in turn requires a hollow tailstock and a ring centre. The second is a 25mm 1" lip-and-spur bit about 305mm 12" long with a threaded

spur (Ridgway call this an auger, too).

The third is a piloted four-pronged driving centre, and the fourth a thread-cutting kit (a Sarjent's screw box and tap). I am assuming you already have a 25mm 1" pin chuck.

I hope I haven't put you off,

Photo 20 The finished music stand.

'It doesn't help when your nearest and dearest says, "*How* much did you pay for that?"'

Geoff Heath is a self-taught amateur turner who has been slowly improving his skills during the past 16 years. Starting with a very small Arundel lathe and a boxed set of three basic tools, he moved on to a Tyme Cub, and now owns a Coronet No 3.

He undertakes small commissions and also sells his work through three local shops and at two craft fairs a year.

In 1988, he retired from his employment as Chief Structural Engineer of the Manchester unit of British Aerospace, so he is fortunate in having plenty of spare time to indulge in his favourite hobby.

He enjoys solving problems, especially ones which involve some mathematics. He has also been known to devise mathematical puzzles.

Geoff's approach to turning is conditioned by his working life as an engineer concerned with the structural integrity of new aircraft designs. In the aircraft industry, design backed by research, and proved by analysis and test, precedes any production, and Geoff finds it natural to adopt this approach to his turning.

Besides being a member of the AWGB, Geoff is a Chartered Engineer, a Fellow of the Institution of Mechanical Engineers and a Fellow of the Royal Aeronautical Society.

but it's only fair to warn you that your pocket may suffer if you have a go.

The spine is the biggest part of the stand. The trick in making this is to drill a 25mm 1" hole down the centre to start. "Put the hole in first, and then you know where it is," is a wise saying I read somewhere.

I started with wood 430mm 17" long x 55mm 2¼" square, which I reduced to an octagon on the bandsaw. Apart from making the roughing out easier, the octagonal shape had another use, which will become apparent later.

My first attempt to drill the hole was unsuccessful. I drilled from each end in turn, but they were slightly out of line, creating a step where they met. It's a good job I wasn't engaged on the Channel Tunnel.

I decided to put a pilot hole through first, and this is where the 8mm ⁵⁄₁₆" auger came in. If you have ever made a standard lamp you will know how to use one.

The right hand end of the workpiece is supported on a ring centre and the auger pushed in through the tailstock. Remove frequently to clear the debris.

At the halfway stage, the workpiece is reversed end to end and the normal driving centre replaced by the piloted version. This fits snugly into the 8mm ⁵⁄₁₆" hole. The boring is then complete.

By good fortune, the threaded spur on my 25mm 1" bit had a maximum diameter of 8mm ⁵⁄₁₆", so the bit was fed along the

pilot hole by advancing the tailstock without any snatching from the spur.

Again, the drilling took place from each end in turn (Photo 2). For the first half, the drive was piloted by the driving centre, but for the second half I had to use a 25mm 1" pin chuck. This time, the two holes met quite accurately.

At the top of the spine is a screw to clamp the sliding rod in position. Before going on, I felt it best to drill and tap the hole for this.

For one thing, there was some extra wall thickness, giving the tap a chance to bite successfully. But the main reason was to use one of the flats of the octagon as a datum when drilling the pilot hole. Now you see the reason for cutting an octagon.

A square section would not have worked so well because tapped holes need to be at right angles to the grain. In other words, they should be drilled radially towards the centre of the wood. Otherwise, the thread is a crumbly mess.

Unless the original square is quarter sawn, an extra set of facets is needed to ensure one pair are more or less parallel to the grain.

The pilot hole was located about 25mm 1" from the top of the spine and was drilled 10mm ³⁄₈" DIA. A 12mm ½" tap was then used to thread the hole.

After all this preparation, it was time to do some turning. I made the biggest diameter 50mm 2" at the top of the spine and 38mm 1½" elsewhere,

except for the fillet at the bottom and the decorative bead in the middle (Photo 3).

Photo 3 The finished spine. Note the tapped hole at the upper (driven) end.

The 'pelvis' section sounds anatomical, but what else can you call the piece joining the legs to the spine? I needed wood about 90mm 3½" square, and had to glue two thinner pieces together to make up the required thickness.

A hexagon rather than an octagon was wanted (Photo 4). Using dividers, I marked out the desired shape on the end of the block, after which it was cut on the bandsaw. Why a hexagon? Because the stand has three legs. Still not clear? Read on! ▶

Photo 4 The hexagonal block for the pelvis.

Photo 2 Drilling the spine on the lathe.

The block — about 150mm 6" long — was mounted between centres and the end next to the tailstock turned almost to a point, so the piece looked like the stub of a giant pencil (Photo 5).

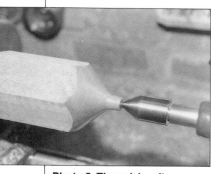

Photo 5 The pelvis, after turning the tapered end.

Photo 6 The pelvis in the drill jig.

I had a simple jig prepared to support the block, angled at 45 DEG, under the bench drill, so that the upper surface of the pointed end was horizontal (Photo 6).

I was now able to drill three holes in the pointed end, using alternate facets of the hexagon as a means of locating them accurately. Now you see why it had to be a hexagon.

Photo 7 An insert being tapped before parting off. The lathe is stationary for this.

However, for the reasons given above, I did not want to tap directly into the block. Instead, I prepared three cross-grained discs of beech each 25mm 1" DIA.

These were drilled and tapped in the lathe (Photo 7), before reducing them to their finished diameter and parting off.

The pelvis was then drilled with a 25mm 1" hole, after which the first disc was glued into place. The block was rotated through 120 DEG, the second hole drilled and filled, and then the third.

As there was some interference between the holes in the middle of the block, the progressive filling and drilling ensured a clean hole was produced for each insert.

Care was taken to sink the face of each insert slightly below the pelvis's surface. The pelvis then went back in the lathe for turning to its final shape (Photo 8), avoiding the area around the inserts so as not to chip the edges of the 25mm 1" holes.

Photo 8 Finished pelvis. The spigot was later shortened.

The upper (driven) end of the pelvis was turned down to a spigot which was a snug fit inside the lower end of the spine. These two components were then glued together.

At the top of the spine is the head. This could have been turned with the neck — a 25mm 1" rod about 405mm 16" long — in one piece, but this would have been wasteful, especially if I had made a mistake during turning. It happens!

You will have gathered that I turned the rod at an earlier stage, to check its fit inside the spine before the pelvis was fitted. The head started as an octagon, which was drilled crossways about 25mm 1" from the top with a 10mm 3/8" hole.

This was later enlarged to 50mm 1/2" through half the thickness before the smaller bore was tapped 50mm 1/2".

So there was a clearance hole halfway through the block, and a tapped hole through the rest.

The head was bored on the lathe with a shallow hole of 25mm 1" DIA to take the neck

Photo 9 Head being drilled for the neck.

Photo 10 Cutting the slot in the head on the bandsaw.

ensure the head kept its alignment, while the slot was cut on the bandsaw (Photo 10).

This operation automatically removed the pip. After the slot had been cleaned, the head and neck were glued together (Photo 11).

Photo 11 Head and neck, with clamping screw.

(Photo 9). By reversing the workpiece and driving it by a pin chuck I was able to turn the top of the head to a hemispherical shape with a small pip at the tailstock end.

After removing from the lathe, the head was slotted centrally, the slot being at right angles to the tapped hole and 12mm 1/2" wide.

A dummy peg screwed into the tapped hole was supported on a block of scrap wood to

Each of the three legs started life as a square section 330mm 13" long, being turned to 25mm 1" DIA at the upper end. Before turning began, the leg was bored for a short distance with a 12mm 1/2" drill (Photo 12), and the resulting hole occupied by the revolving centre (Photo 13).

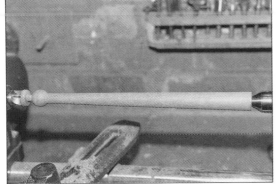

Photo 12 Drilling a leg for its threaded spigot.

Photo 13 A finished leg.

This hole later accommodated a threaded spigot. The leg tapered towards the bottom, ending in a ball about 22mm ⁷⁄₈″ DIA. After taking from the lathe, the bottom end was cleaned up by removing the driving pip.

Three small lengths of beech were then turned to 12mm ½″ DIA, leaving the driven end square and slightly tapering the other end (Photo 14).

Photo 14 A leg spigot after turning.

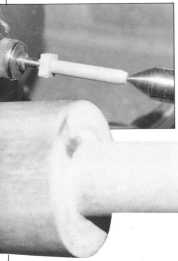

These were threaded using a Sarjent's box. The square end helped give a good grip during this process. Note that you can't thread all the way down a dowel by this method. There will always be a short length of plain shaft left (Photo 15).

While using the screw box,

the clamping screws were made by threading two short lengths of beech and gluing them into turned knobs.

Photo 15 The spigot after threading.

One screw — with no plain shank exposed — clamped the neck at the desired height in the spine, while the other (with 25mm 1″ of plain shank exposed) squeezed the slot in the head to lock the music desk at the required angle (Photo 16).

After cutting off their tapered 'starters' and square ends, the threaded dowels were screwed into the pelvis and the legs pushed home (but not glued) on to the plain shanks.

Now came the moment of truth. Would the spine stand vertically? Not quite, and slivers of packing were placed under two legs until the spine was upright.

The unpacked leg clearly needed most adjustment, and had to be shortened by the square root of two (= 1.414) times the thickness of the thicker packing, since the leg

was angled at 45 DEG to the vertical.

It was shortened on the lathe, driving the ball end through a simple cup chuck and cutting back the upper end without quite touching the revolving centre with the parting off tool.

The second leg was shortened by an amount equal to the square root of two times the difference between the thicknesses of the two packers. The third leg was left alone.

Once the legs had been adjusted in this way and the sit of the stand re-checked, the dowels were glued into the legs.

The tips of the threaded spigots and the surfaces of the inserts in the pelvis were colour-coded to ensure the legs were correctly assembled.

I was dismayed to find the legs needed this adjustment, but it became clear that any

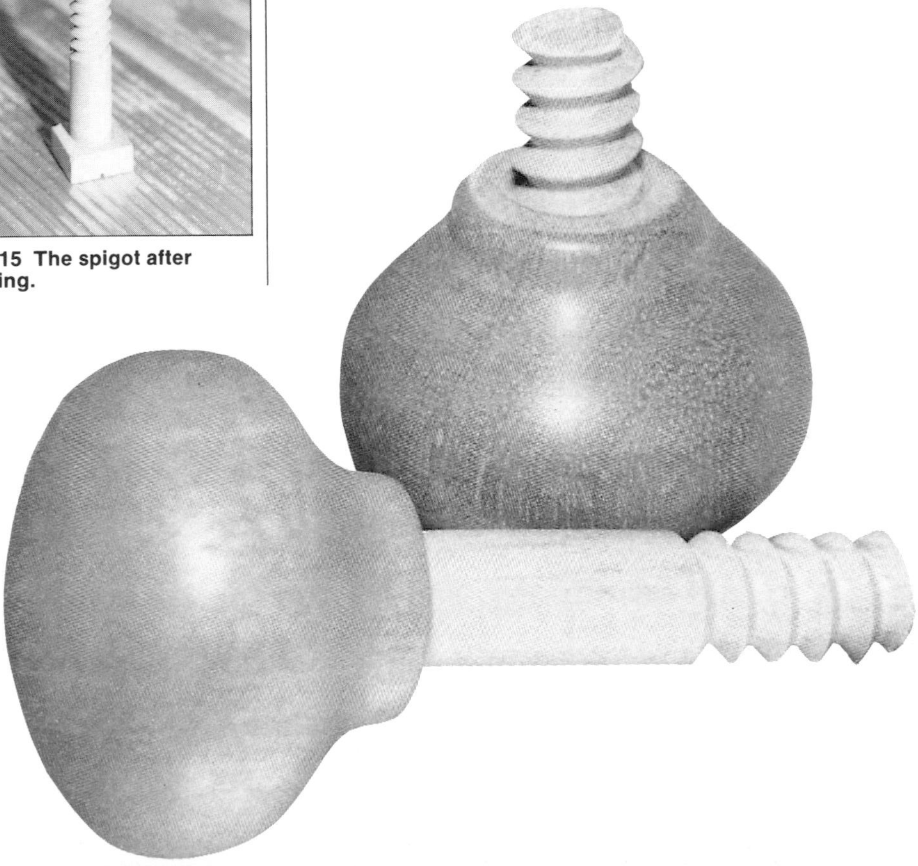

▶

Photo 16 The two clamping screws.

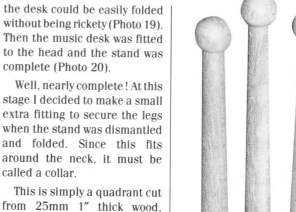

Photo 18 One of the two lower edges of the music stand.

small differences in their splay angles, in the setting of the inserts in the spine, or inaccuracies in the shaping and centring of the hexagon, would call for compensating alterations to the legs.

I nearly didn't confess my errors, but as the photos show the differing leg lengths only too clearly, I decided to come clean.

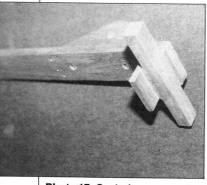

Photo 17 Central component of the music desk.

The turning was now finished, and the more mundane work (for a turner) of making the music stand, could begin. The central feature is a slab 50mm 2" wide x 330mm 13" long x 10mm ⅜" thick.

This carries a bracket on its rear face which fits snugly into the head slot, being supported on the shank of the clamping screw (Photo 17).

The front of the slab has a cross-bar 125mm 5" long x 20mm ¾" x 12mm ½". This serves as a stop to prevent the desk from folding downwards.

It is screwed to the slab through a 5mm 3⁄16" packer to allow for the thickness of the bottom rail.

Each half of the bottom rail carries a short length of plastic channel section which fits over the cross-bar, stopping the desk distorting from its plane.

The rest of the desk consists of a series of strips, each 20mm ¾" wide x 5mm 3⁄16" thick, pivoted at their extremities on countersunk bolts fitted with locknuts to form a parallelogram. The lowest strip is wider (45mm 1¾") and carries the music sheet ledge, beneath which are strengthening corner blocks of plastic channels (Photo 18).

Photo 19 The assembled music desk, partly folded.

The cross-bar carries a short fill-in piece to close the central gap in the ledge.

The nuts were tightened until

the desk could be easily folded without being rickety (Photo 19). Then the music desk was fitted to the head and the stand was complete (Photo 20).

Well, nearly complete! At this stage I decided to make a small extra fitting to secure the legs when the stand was dismantled and folded. Since this fits around the neck, it must be called a collar.

This is simply a quadrant cut from 25mm 1" thick wood, drilled with a 25mm 1" hole to slip over the neck, and with

Photo 21 The collar.

three tapped holes on a 75mm 3" radius (Photo 21).

When the legs are removed from the pelvis, they are

Photo 22 Legs screwed into the collar.

screwed into the collar (Photo 22), which then goes over the neck.

The head is clamped down on to the collar and the desk is folded down over the spine. The whole thing is easily carried about without losing any of the pieces. ■

Photo 23 The folded stand.

JAN SANDERS

Jan Sanders was one of three pupils on Toby Kaye's first course on making a sounding bowl. She reports here on her findings.

Singing BOWLS

Toby Kaye, Wilma and Christopher with a deep, organic sounding bowl made by Toby.

Bernard Maunder's sounding bowl.

The week stretched blissfully ahead. No pressures, no commitments other than to pay attention and do as I was asked. In short, a woodturner's holiday.

Among Toby Kaye's opening remarks at this five-day course into making what I call a 'musical bowl' was a quote from David Pye: ''A bowl will be forever silent or sing where it stands . . .'' The depth of this observation came to mind throughout the week.

We three course members were each allocated a lathe in a workshop warmed by a fan suspended above a sawdust burner. The day started with a big decision — should I make a deep, organic-looking bowl turned in at the rim, or tackle a larger diameter, shallower bowl?

Toby showed us fine examples of both varieties in a portfolio bursting with beautiful pieces, each singing out of the pages. Using an unusual amount of discretion, I opted for the more familiar form of the open bowl.

The wisdom of this choice became clear later,

when John Taylor's bowl came to grief during the hollowing out stage. So it was shallow bowls for all of us.

I selected a large lump of sugar maple, partly air-dried, from Toby's woodstore, which looks like a garden cold frame. The maple had a softish patch but was, hopefully, not too far gone.

The blank measured 485mm 19″ DIA x 100mm 4″, which I mounted with a faceplate outboard on the long-bed Harrison Graduate. Going down on bended knee for more reasons than one, I made sure I was using the slowest RPM.

After truing the blank and making a recess for

▶

'The course is not for beginners or the faint-hearted but for those with well practiced basic skills and an interest in the unusual.'

Born in West
Hartlepool, Jan
Sanders first
contemplated a
career in agriculture.
After leaving
agricultural college,
she ran a
smallholding, later
supplying shops with
craft items made from
straw plaiting, willow
basket weaving and
woodturning.

Jan was taught
woodturning by her
future husband, John,
who had his own
woodturner's
business near Chard,
Somerset, and
needed extra help.
The couple are
members of the
Worshipful Company
of Turners.

John, a freelance
teacher in
woodturning, who
runs courses at
Yandles and helped
Toby Kaye develop
his teaching skills,
was formerly a
Professor at the
British Academy of
Fencing.

He was the South
West's fencing coach
for over 40 years.

The couple have an
interest in two shops
— *Makers*, a
cooperative run by 10
craftspeople in
Taunton, and a
showroom (shared
with a potter) at the
Cricket St. Thomas
Wildlife Park, near
Chard.

Jan uses the water lily
as a main motif, and
some of her
woodturnings
also include
willow
weaving.
Colours
are a
feature
of her
work,
and she
has started
writing a
book on
this.

Most of Jan's work
is sold in the South
West, but she also
supplies galleries in
America, London and
the Scilly Isles. She
has two children and
two step children.

the expanding collet chuck, leaving a 125mm 5″ DIA bottom upon which the bowl could finally rest, I embarked upon the long, slow curve towards the outer rim (FIG 1). The bowl's greatest diameter is 15mm ⅝″ below the rim.

From past experience, I knew it would be wise to make all my cuts finishing ones. In this way, it is possible to avoid the trauma of the finishing cut itself. You simply stop work when the required shape is reached.

Powder sanding was followed with a coat made from a mixture of beeswax, carnauba wax and boiled linseed oil. This buffed to a pleasing satin finish.

I reversed the piece on to an expanding collet

chuck, shaping the rim to accommodate the string retaining pegs, the tuning pins and the brass sleeves through which the strings pass on both sides of the bowl.

The rim is undercut using a short bevelled deep-fluted gouge (FIG 2). Strength is needed at the outer edge to withstand the strain of the taught strings, but the tone of the completed bowl is reflected by the inside curve and thickness of wood, especially in the bottom of the bowl.

During the hollowing process, thanks to Toby's sensitive demonstration and encouragement, I

FIG 2 Profile of rim and undercut.

FIG 1 The long, slow curve towards the outer rim, 485mm 19″ DIA.

John Taylor's completed bowl.

The tone of the completed bowl is reflected by the inside curve and thickness of wood.

Adjusting and readjusting the position of the eight strings.

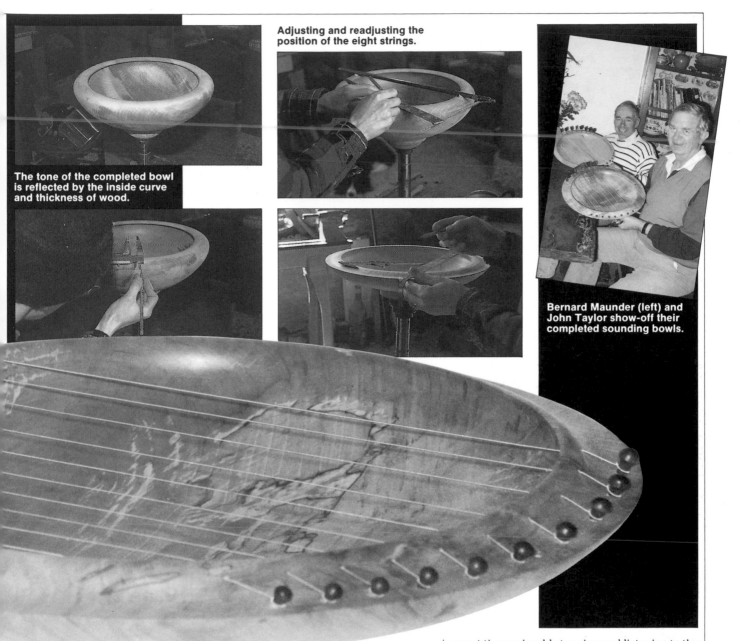

Bernard Maunder (left) and John Taylor show-off their completed sounding bowls.

Sugar maple sounding bowl 485mm 19" x 100mm 4" made by Jan Sanders in 1993.

'Among Toby's opening words at this five-day course was a quote from David Pye: "A bowl will be forever silent or sing where it stands."'

Drilling the holes to carry the brass sleeves.

spent time enjoyably tapping and listening to the changing timbre of the wood, a moving and satisfying experience.

After completing the inside and admiring nature's patterns, I reversed the bowl once more, this time holding it with Toby's special expanding wooden jaws. The other two, slightly smaller bowls, were remounted on a jam fit chuck.

I considerably reduced the plinth on which the bowl rested, blending the recess but leaving just enough flat on which it could stand. This also meant thinning the bowl's centre. Tapping created incredibly light responses.

The bowl was now complete and Toby seemed pleased with its potential as a musical instrument, although there was still a long way to go. In fact we were only half way through the course.

Then followed the most technical part, which stretched Toby's teaching skills and mine as a

▶

student. Mental arithmetic gave way to the calculator as we adjusted and readjusted the measurements for the positioning of the eight strings.

Far from the difficulties of making them equidistant from one another, we had fun grading the gaps between the strings. The finest and highest pitched string is about 20mm ¾" away from the 45mm 1¾" wide rim. The heaviest and lowest note string lies just to the far side of the bowl's centre.

Using Toby's formula and double checking every angle, mark and measurement, we nervously drilled the holes to carry the brass sleeves on either side of the bowl.

We had to bear in mind that the hole diameters are drilled to suit the various sleeve sizes. The sleeving is superglued in place and, as the largest is a mere 1.8mm outside diameter, the job calls for some dexterity.

Tapered holes for the string retaining pegs were drilled on one side of the rim and similar holes for the tuning pins on the other. We learnt how to make a tapered bit with which to drill these holes.

A contrasting wood was chosen for the pegs, which looked like round headed golf tees (FIG 3). The skill was in making the peg's taper match that of the hole.

Inserting the zither pins used for turning.

The sleeving is superglued in place.

Jan Sanders' 'musical bowl'.

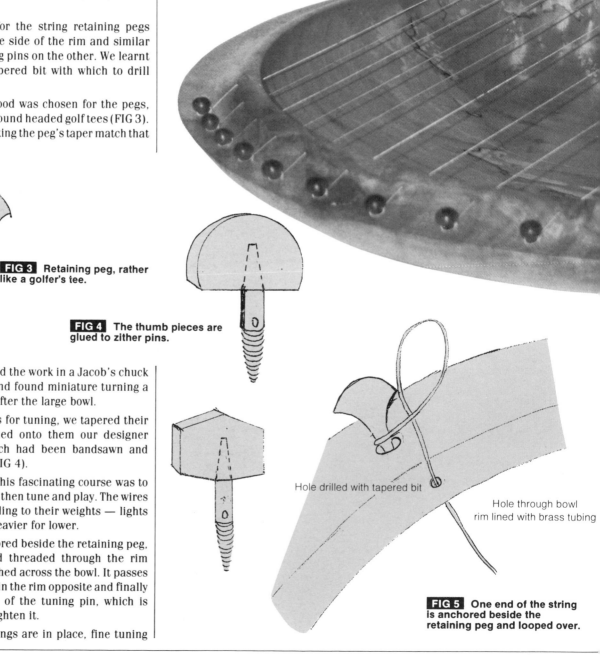

FIG 3 Retaining peg, rather like a golfer's tee.

FIG 4 The thumb pieces are glued to zither pins.

To do this we held the work in a Jacob's chuck in the headstock and found miniature turning a pleasant contrast after the large bowl.

Using zither pins for tuning, we tapered their tops and superglued onto them our designer thumb pieces which had been bandsawn and sanded to shape (FIG 4).

The final lap of this fascinating course was to string the bowl and then tune and play. The wires are selected according to their weights — lights for higher notes, heavier for lower.

One end is anchored beside the retaining peg, looped over it and threaded through the rim before being stretched across the bowl. It passes through the sleeve in the rim opposite and finally through the shank of the tuning pin, which is screwed down to tighten it.

When all the strings are in place, fine tuning

Hole drilled with tapered bit

Hole through bowl rim lined with brass tubing

FIG 5 One end of the string is anchored beside the retaining peg and looped over.

Polishing the thumb pieces.

The retaining peg's taper must match that of the hole.

Checking that the zither pins fit into the thumb pieces.

Inserting the wires.

Hammering in the retaining pins.

Thumb pieces are marked out for cutting.

The three course members (left to right) John Taylor, Bernard Maunder and Jan Sanders, proudly display their sounding bowls.

can begin. My bowl carried eight strings and, when tuned to the pentatonic scale and plucked, produced a wonderful mellow tone and deep resonance.

The pentatonic scale has five notes in each octave, a delightful contradiction in terms, but one which describes it perfectly.

The course is not for beginners or the faint-hearted but for those with well practiced basic skills and an interest in the unusual.

It is a very fulfilling experience, coupled with country kitchen lunches by Wilma and breaktime entertainment from the couple's delightful young son, Christopher. Altogether, a marvellous experience.

I am sure Toby enjoyed giving of his knowledge and his new-found teaching skills. He is a thoughtful, profound woodturner, and I felt we really shared creating my bowl, which 'sings where it stands'. ■

See page 64 for Toby Kaye's address.

Chris Pye has been both a professional woodturner and carver over some 16 years. He started with carving, owing his formative introduction to the master woodcarver Gino Masero, and a little later added woodturning.

He considers himself self taught, and equally at home in both crafts, often combining them.

Chris was born in Co. Durham but has lived a large part of his life in the South West of England and currently lives in Bristol.

His carvings are mainly commissioned, and range from lettering and heraldry, figurework and personal sculpture to the restoration of old carvings.

His turned work includes newel posts (up to 2.9 metres 9' 6" long), stair parts, table legs, lamps and knobs for the trade as well as individual bowls and boxes.

Turning and carving are combined in four poster bedposts, barley twists, lettered bowls, columns and one-off pieces.

He has several years' experience teaching adult education classes in woodcarving as well as private students in both turning and carving. In 1990 he demonstrated at the AWGB Seminar at Loughborough. At present he is writing the first of a series of books around the area of carving and turning.

Chris is a Buddhist and is married with two children.

Chris Pye
The Poplars
Ewyas Harold
Hereford
HR2 OHU

A MALLET FROM A WOOD

CHRIS PYE

Chris gives a new meaning to turning a bowl.

One day I arrived at the workshop to find a bowls ball, or wood, and a chisel without a handle on the bench. There were a few lines drawn on a piece of wood with a request from a friend to make a carving mallet out of the bowls wood and a handle for the chisel.

As the turning is straightforward, with quite satisfying end results, these two jobs make useful, basic projects.

In my work as a carver I know there are definite features that make a good mallet shape, and others that decide whether a handle works or not. These details need to be considered carefully right at the beginning, so I will start by describing what is needed. Then I will run through the process of making the items.

If you have friends who carve, this could be an area where you, as a turner, could help them. If nothing else you can impress your friends with your subtle knowledge. You may even get paid! And with the increasing use of carving tools on turnings, you may need this information yourself.

In this issue I will deal with the mallet. Woodcarver's mallets are round, not square. There are definite reasons why this shape is preferred. The earliest known mallets, Egyptian, were made quite naturally from branches of heavy wood waisted for a handle.

Square billets of wood, again with an integral handle, are shown in Roman paintings but being used for mortising, not carving as they still are today.

So both round and square-headed mallets have a very long history, continuing up to the present time, and each has its own place. But why the different shapes?

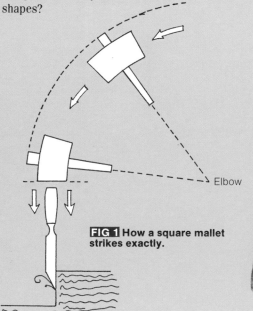

Photo 1 Various mallets in my workshop. The one top right is nylon, and far right is a mild steel one, used with an end ferrule on the carving gouge.

FIG 1 How a square mallet strikes exactly.

Elbow

When you are chopping in a woodworking joint, say a mortise, the flat side of the chisel forms its own guiding jig as it cuts. To keep the true face of the joint, the chisel needs to be struck squarely. Hence the need for the square, flat face of the mallet (FIG 1).

A carving gouge, on the other hand, is struck from all sorts of directions, being offered to the wood at an infinite number of angles. The force in this case is transmitted tangentially (FIG 2)

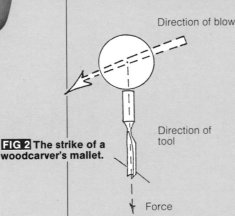

FIG 2 The strike of a woodcarver's mallet.

Direction of blow

Direction of tool

Force

and the mallet does not have to be aligned in the same, exact way. Carvers tend to collect a variety of mallets for different jobs (Photo 1).

Mallets with separate handles are relatively recent, probably stemming from when newly-discovered and dense woods, such as lignum vitae, could be exploited for their weight and size ratios.

Lignum is one of the best woods to use, as the diameter of the mallet does not become too big where, say, a beech mallet

'If nothing else you can impress your carving friends with your subtle knowledge.'

must be considerably larger to get a similar weight.

I also use other materials such as nylon and mild steel. (I must confess — the nylon one is my favourite!)

Bowls woods, used on grass and made from lignum, are

becoming easier to obtain from bowls clubs as there is a tendency to move to ones made from artificial materials which are unaffected by the weather.

The Shape. You can see that the shape is round in cross section. The head is also slightly tapered towards the handle because, like the square mallet, the blow pivots from the elbow.

The tapering head of the mallet allows it to strike the handle of a cutting tool more precisely, at least in the one direction. A slight belly at the striking point also helps strengthen this part against wear and tear (FIG 3).

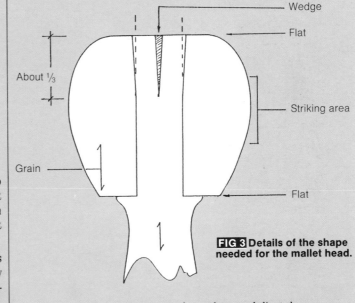

Wedge

Flat

About ⅓

Striking area

Grain

Flat

FIG 3 Details of the shape needed for the mallet head.

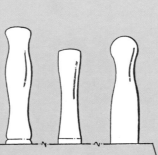

FIG 4 Some possible handle shapes.

The handle needs to fit comfortably in the hand with nothing prominent that can cause blistering. Bear in mind that a mallet may be used all day long, doing a lot of work. Too fat a shape can make the hands ache, too thin and it feels a little weak and uncertain (FIG 4).

The best wood is a straight, close-grained bit of ash or hickory, although other woods such as box or yew work well. Pick something that looks good.

The handle is wedged into the head of the mallet. A very important point is that the hole for the handle needs to taper out a little at the far end. The spigot of the handle, when wedged, becomes locked and immovable. Indeed you have to drill the handle out should you ever need to replace it.

If this tapered fit is not made the head can loosen, even with the wedge. This does not apply so much to smaller mallets used more delicately.

A flat top to the head of the mallet is also needed. This allows it to sit upright on the bench and not roll around.

Tools and Equipment. For making the mallet from the bowls wood you will need the following tools and equipment to follow my instructions: roughing gouge 25mm 1″, skew chisel 10mm ⅜″, parting chisel 10mm ⅜″, straight scraper with a width less than 25mm 1″.

A 4-prong drive centre and revolving tail centre, a G clamp (wider than the diameter of the ball), a 3 or 4-jaw scroll chuck (the bigger the better), a Jacobs chuck for the headstock, and a 25mm 1″ Fostner bit for boring the hole. ▶

You will also need two hardwood wooden plugs for a 25mm 1″ hole with quite a long taper. Leave the surfaces rough to grip better and score lines around them at 2mm ¹⁄₁₆″ intervals. This allows you to align them accurately in the holes. Make these before you begin.

Finally, a spigot to be gripped in the scroll chuck: A piece of hardwood about 100mm 4″ long by 38mm 1½″. Make this when you need it. And for finishing, sandpaper, sealer, and raw linseed oil.

Making the head. Remove the metal caps from either end of the wood using a suicide chisel or screwdriver. You should find the centre of the original lignum vitae tree underneath these caps. It is down the centre we will pass the handle.

There are often hairline splits that can be ignored as they do not affect the performance of the mallet.

Saw off a small facet on opposite sides of the ball to allow you to grip it better in the following operations (Photo 2).

I used the band saw, but cutting a sphere like this is not the safest operation, so go slowly without undue pressure and allow the blade to do the work.

Keep your fingers clear and never direct your hand directly towards the blade, always feeding wood at a parallel line to the cut. If you are not happy with this a good vice and handsaw will do.

Thump the 4-pronged drive centre into each end to mark them.

Don't forget, before you start raising lignum vitae dust you must protect yourself from it adequately.

With the ball supported by the tailstock centre, bore the hole from the headstock end. Clamp across the facets on the ball and rest the clamp on the tool rest. This will stop the ball turning as you bore (Photo 3).

Photo 2 Bandsawing two facets on the sides of the wood.

Photo 8 The head held by the spigot in the 3-jaw chuck.

Photo 3 Using the G clamp to hold the wood while boring.

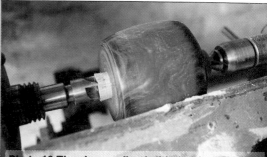
Photo 9 Reaming the wedge end of the hole. A few strokes will probably be enough.

Photo 4 Plug in position, boring from the other end.

Photo 10 The shape refined with the skew chisel.

Photo 5 Roughing to shape.

Photo 11 The spigot formed in the handle.

Photo 6 Starting to work the ends. Note the cylinder of wood left around the plug.

Photo 12 A coat of sealer.

Photo 7 Checking flatness of the ends with a straight edge.

Photo 13 Bandsawing a kerf in the handle spigot to take the wedge.

Photo 14 Tapping home the wedge.

'An occasional wipe with linseed oil will keep it sweet, though don't try this with the owner!'

Photo 15 End view of the mallet showing the flat face, the wedge and some hairline shakes radiating from the centre of the original tree or branch.

With a slow speed, and taking it easy, bore to about 20mm ¾″ from the other end. You can use masking tape to mark this depth on the bit.

Tap a plug squarely into the hole. Reverse the ball and finish boring through to the first hole (Photo 4).

Tap a second plug in accurately and mount between centres. Rough the ball to the maximum diameter (Photo 5). Bring the tool rest in closer and mark the required length at each end with a pencil line.

The next step is to completely square off the ends to the pencil lines. Now, if you merrily cut down to the plugs, you will cut through to the plug at a smaller diameter than that which is supporting the hole: the plug will loosen and the work may disengage the centre, coming off the lathe altogether.

There is a trick to doing this with the plugs in: Take the ends of the cylinder down to 38mm 1½″ DIA with the parting tool, leaving therefore only 3mm ⅛″ of thickness to remove (Photo 6).

Using the long point of the skew chisel take off no more than 2mm ¹⁄₁₆″ of wood at a time from the ends, scoring into the plug. As you reduce the length of lignum *wind in the tailstock and take up the slack that is produced.*

A cut, then a tightening up. In this way the plug is continuously worked into the hole and there is no danger of the work coming off.

Use the skew to pare the ends up to the lines, making them parallel. The top will then sit on the bench, and the bottom will meet the shoulder of the handle. Check them with a straight edge (Photo 7).

Take the ball off the lathe and remove the plugs — a Stilson wrench or Mole grip may be useful here.

Make a hardwood spigot of a diameter that taps nicely into whichever of the 25mm 1″ holes you have decided is the handle end of the mallet.

The spigot should enter the hole to a depth of about a third of the way into the ball. Lignum, although withstanding compression amazingly, will split more easily, so take care when inserting the spigot not to over-force it.

Trial and error here will give you enough of a snug fit so that you can hold the ball when the other end of the spigot is gripped by the 3-jaw scroll chuck (Photo 8).

To get the ball aligned, use the tailstock to push the mallet head tight up against the jaws of the chuck before tightening them well. You should now have freedom to work the wedge-end hole.

Using a slow speed and light strokes with the straight side scraper (Photo 9) ream out the hole. Increase the diameter of the hole by only 3mm ⅛″ at the exit, starting from a depth of about one third of the way in. This is enough!

Replace the plugs. Line up the ball on the lathe and shape it with the skew chisel (Photo 10).

Finish by sanding to at least 180 grit, and enjoy it — the surface will not look so nice for long, once it starts being used!

Polish in a coat or two of linseed oil. I used raw linseed, but boiled linseed oil can be thinned a little with turpentine.

The head is now finished and can be removed from the lathe.

Making the Handle. The handle is turned as a normal bit of between centres work (Photo 11).

Make the spigot that goes through the head about 6mm ¼″ over length and a snug fit. Undercut the shoulder slightly.

Feel the handle for comfort — you can take it off the lathe and try it with the head on to get the right shape.

Finish well and seal it, say with a coat of cellulose lacquer finely cut back (Photo 12) but don't end up with a shiny, slippery surface. Leave the end blips on for the time being.

Make a support (Photo 13) so that the spigot can be offered to the bandsaw safely and accurately, and saw down the centre about two thirds of the way.

Make the wedge long and slender. A different coloured bit of hardwood, in this case walnut, looks well.

Assembly. Insert the spigot making sure the shoulder of the handle is flush against the head. Stand the handle on end on the bench and drive the wedge home (Photo 14).

Trim off the wedge and spigot end with a small saw and chisel, and sandpaper smooth.

The wedge causes the end of the handle to expand into an elliptical shape within a round hole, so you will see a little gap appear at the sides. Fill this with wax (Photo 15). Trim off the blip at the other end of the handle, sand and seal as before.

The mallet is now finished. It should reside, like all wood, away from direct sources of heat. An occasional wipe with linseed oil will keep it sweet, though don't try this with the owner!

Now you will be looking for something to thump with it. In the article on page 116 I show you how the handle for the chisel was made. ■

Within every acorn an oak tree

TOBIAS KAYE

In this intriguing project for a turned acorn with interior space, Tobias Kaye shares the secrets of his involuted or inside -out turning technique.

Tobias Kaye worked in forestry, computing and education before becoming a full time professional woodturner and setting up his first workshop at Stroud in 1982. He moved to his present base in Devon three years later.

His work has always been widely varied, from furniture parts and architectural turning to one-off artistic pieces, especially bowls. For the past seven years he has been designing and turning legs and finials for a top British furniture manufacturer, and he also acts as a consultant to woodturning equipment manufacturers.

In 1986 he started turning acoustically formed wooden bowls to which he fitted musical strings. He has since made more than 30 of his musical 'sounding bowls'. Two years ago he began experimenting with the involuted turning technique shown in this project.

Tobias is a founder member of the AWGB, and of the Green Woodturners group dedicated to raising awareness of ecological issues. His work has been selected for quality by The Worshipful Company of Turners and he is on the Crafts Council register.

He has held numerous exhibitions in both the UK and abroad, he frequently demonstrates around the UK, and runs a series of courses on various aspects of woodturning.

Tobias Kaye, Whites Cross, 10 Lower Dean, Buckfastleigh, Devon TQ11 0LS. Tel: 0364 42837.

This design for a turned acorn is adapted from the finial on a gatepost of a rather fine house I once visited. The outside form is pretty much the same, but the windows and interior spaces are created using an involuted turning technique a furniture designer friend and I developed from an idea given at the 1989 International Woodturning Seminar at Loughborough by Del Stubbs.

During a slide show of various pieces, Del showed a shot of a signpost he had turned, cut in four down its length and reassembled inside out after the technique created by Stephen Hogbin, the Canadian sculptor/turner.

The two developments my furniture designer friend and I added to this is first, turning the reassembled piece a second time as opposed to leaving its outer surfaces square as Hogbin and Stubbs had done. Second is planning the window shapes to the degree that their design becomes an integral part of the overall design, harmonious with the whole, rather than the haphazard result of cutting something designed in the round. Planned finished shapes were of course part of Hogbin's sculptures but the outsides were, as far as I know, left square.

This design arose when I was casting around for a piece to produce at a demonstration in Plymouth for nearly 200 people. I needed something I could produce in under 1½ hours, would capture the imagination, and had potential for amusement.

Pencil and paper are useful for planning these turnings as the relationship between window forms and outside forms is too complex for me to juggle using mind alone. I have since used it in many demonstrations and offer it as one option to people who come on some of my woodturning courses.

The reasons this design pleases me so much are that the fully grown oak tree in the top window is contained within an acorn, and the acorn-shaped window below appears to be underground as if the tree above had sprung from it.

The star shape below symbolises rock crystal to represent the mineral world that supports the plant life such as trees which have such a patient and essential role in supporting life on earth.

Leaving the outside form square at the base also has this effect of symbolising the earth. Such a square base is an integral part of giving a solid foundation to many turned designs. Straight lines for strength, curves for warmth and for elegance — fundamental principles of design.

There are two further methods

of preparing the initial block. Either one piece can be planed to exact squareness, or four exactly square planed pieces can be taped up to make a block. You can buy joinery pine ready planed. Usually its squareness is exact but take a set square with you and check before you buy.

This piece is made from 125mm x 125mm 5″ x 5″ Douglas fir as that is what I had hanging around. The dimensions on the sketch can be converted using a calculator to suit a block of four pieces of 50mm 2″ nominal (45mm 1¾″ finished) joinery pine by dividing each figure by 1.425, writing in the resultant dimensions and working to these. Leave 25mm 1″ waste at either end.

I made two mistakes. First, I chose Douglas fir which does not turn cleanly. Some of the cuts on this design are tricky and a wood that automatically comes clean off the chisel is an advantage. I suggest a smooth grained wood like sycamore, lime, poplar or walnut would be suitable. Harder timbers like cherry and beech are less suitable.

Second, I made the oak tree too wide which meant that the top part of the acorn became too fat for its length giving the whole piece a dumpy look. During the first stage of turning be careful not to go too deep in the tree pattern and this will not happen.

If you are planing up your own block of timber, make sure

precisely. This is best done with a marking gauge as corner to corner measurements are less easy to get exact.

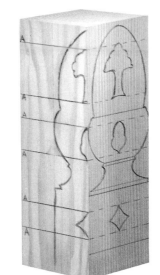

Photo 1 The design is drawn on one face and squared and measured round the block to create the depthing line on the next side.

Now draw the finished item onto one side of the wood (FIG 1 and Photo 1) allowing waste top and bottom. Using a set square, mark a strong line at the top and bottom of each window. Square these lines round onto the next face and, to help you visualise what you are going to turn, sketch the inside out version of that onto this face (FIG 2 and Photo 1). This line of

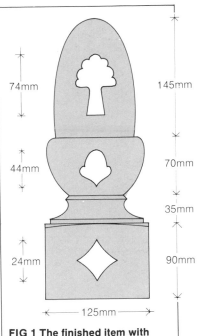

FIG 1 The finished item with dimensions in mm for a block measuring 125mm x 125mm x 380mm 5″ x 5″ x 15″.

from the square face in, is equal to half the width of the finished window.

Rule two is: measure this depth in from the point at which the depthing line is marked onto the square face.

It has taken me a long time of making, thinking and making again to arrive at these two simple rules. The second rule has been vastly simplified by the use of the depthing line so draw this accurately.

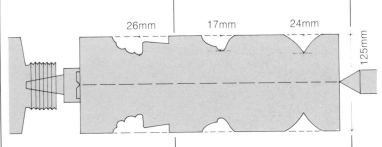

FIG 2 Side view of the first stage of turning showing depth of cuts in mm.

it is truly square at every corner. These corners are going to be turned into the centre and will only fit together without gaps if every one of them is exactly square. The next step is to mark the centre of both ends

half the design is called the depthing line, and is drawn as follows.

The calculation of the depth of each part of the first stage of turning this piece is quite simple. Rule one is: the depth

I only discovered this rule during the writing of this article. It is because I did not apply it to making this acorn that the top part is too fat for its length on the finished item.

Having gone too deep in making the tree by not measuring from the depthing line, the size of the final stage tree window disallowed my▶

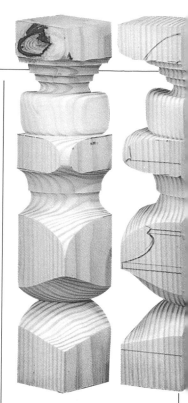

Photo 2 Measuring the depth of the window with callipers. Ideally these should be held against a straight edge running across the position of the depthing line.

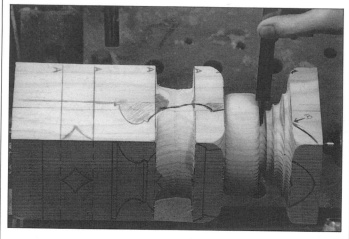

making the finished top section as slender as it is in the original drawing.

Photo 2 shows me using vernier callipers and sighting across the flat to measure the depth. If I had held a straight edge across where the depthing line had been and measured in from there I would not have gone so deep.

You do not need to know these two rules to make this project because I will give you all the dimensions, but I set the rules out as an aid to designing your own involuted project after completing this one. On my courses I lay these principles out in three dimensions, with examples you can hold, making them even easier to understand.

Square lines

Having marked out the two sides of the block, mount it between centres and start the lathe. You should see the square across lines that mark the ends of the windows stand out visibly while the work is spinning. If not, stop and mark them on again with a soft pencil or a ballpoint pen using the set square. These are the lines marked. A in Photo 1.

Now begin to cut between these lines. Don't cut any wood off the parts not due to become windows. Cut the window parts

down to round using either a long pointed gouge or a skew chisel and stop the lathe again.

At this point you can think that if you leave the shoulders where unturned wood meets turned parts straight, or square, the effect in the finished piece

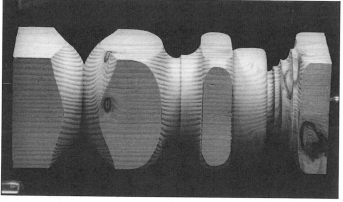

Photo 3 The first stage turning completed.

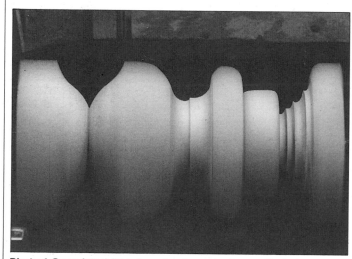

Photo 4 Completed first stage turning spinning on the lathe.

will be a flat surface. This might be desirable in some designs, but it will show up your glue lines and any defects in the joinery.

In this design I wanted the base inside each window to curve away out of sight, mainly to form a link between each part of the pattern, but also to hide the joints. Also, if you want a lamp cord up the middle of any design, all you have to do is turn away the outermost 6mm ¼" of the square at this stage over the whole length to leave a hole up the middle.

A cord hanging down the middle tends to be a distraction from the harmony of the pattern. Perhaps the best way to overcome this is to turn a long thin tube with features that harmonise with the window shapes. To fit this you must drill out before final gluing takes place, holding the involuted block together with double sided tape.

Meanwhile, back on the lathe, turn in the tree pattern (FIG 2) to the marked depth. Use vernier callipers to measure the depth of your cutting before you go too deep. Be careful to measure in from your depthing line.

Turn back the corners similarly (Photos 3 and 4). Now turn in the shapes of the other windows. Take care that the sharp points of the windows are nice and clean, especially the root points at the base of the trunks of the tree and the deepest point of the star-crystal design.

Use your best skills and very sharp tools to get a good finish. Sand only those parts of the turning that are fully round. If you sand the edges of the parts left square they will no longer meet up when reassembled.

A little hand sanding can be done on these parts with the lathe stationary, so long as the abrasive moves with the grain and does not disturb the edge lines. Now polish the whole of the turned area taking care to allow none to touch the flat surfaces. This completes the first stage of turning.

Next set up the saw with a sharp blade. Mark the centre line of the flat areas with a marking gauge and use this line to set the fence on the saw. Cut

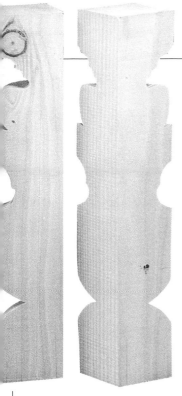

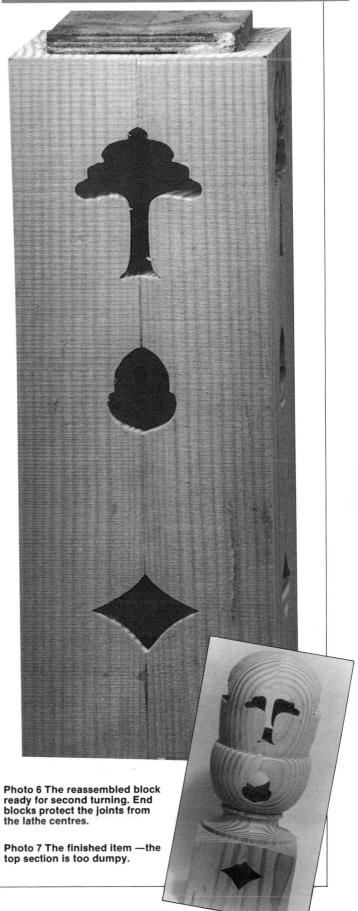

squeezes out onto the interior spaces, you will have a tricky job cleaning it up. If excess glue has to be removed it is best done when the glue has jelled.

When both pairs are glued up it's time to drill for any insert you may want to make. Assemble the pairs, either using double sided tape in the joint, or masking tape around the outside, or with clamps, and drill the holes to accept the centre turning. Disassemble and glue the halves together as normal, making sure the centre lines are matching up.

If you are not making any insert for the centre simply glue up the two halves, carefully matching the window edges.

Now the whole involuted work is assembled, fix a block of ply to both ends using hot melt glue (Photo 6). This is to avoid

Photo 5 The block sawn into quarters and ready to be reassembled.

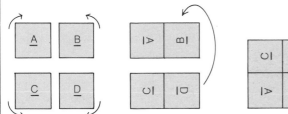
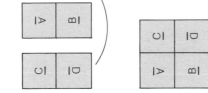

FIG 3 End view of rotating the quarters for perfect book matched grain all round the outside.

down the centre of the line, not to one side of it as you would for joinery. Once in halves, mark these to assist in pairing the quarters (Photo 5 and FIG 3) and saw again.

Take one pair of quarters and roll it back on itself so that which was a flat surface is now two faces of the joint (FIG 3). Practise this several times on both pairs before applying the glue. It's easy to get it wrong and glue up non-matching quarters.

The planed surfaces must be absolutely level with each other for the next stage of joining so hold these down onto a flat surface during gluing or clamping. I use PVA for soft woods and Cascamite for hardwoods. Apply only just enough to join securely. If it

the lathe centres forcing the glue joints open. Scribe centres as before, place in the lathe and turn to the finished shape.

Use sharp tools and light cuts over the windows. Some woods may break away a little at the window edges, so stop and check from time to time. Sand gently at high speed to avoid undue rounding of window edges. If these are left sharp, remove the arrises with very fine abrasive. Polish as before. The square sections can be sanded using a belt, disc or drill mounted sander and polished with a buffer.

Applications of this design are various. You could mount this piece as a finial into a newel post or two of them onto bed headposts. A smaller version could be the handle of a walking stick and a larger version could be a lampstand or even gateposts for a large house. ∎

Photo 6 The reassembled block ready for second turning. End blocks protect the joints from the lathe centres.

Photo 7 The finished item —the top section is too dumpy.

ALEC JARDINE

South African Alec Jardine has found a use for blanks which cracked when he moved to a drier area. Instead of round bowls, he makes them slab-like.

The badly cracked blanks.

Two things have recently led me to experiment with a different style of bowl making. The first was moving from a fairly humid part of the country to a drier area which caused the bowl slabs or billets I had accumulated to crack and distort.

The second was a plea from a friend for some nut bowls which wouldn't blow away at her family's weekly barbecue.

back verandah. I'd been using them to turn large bowls.

When we moved south to Port Elizabeth the blanks, together with other bits and pieces of timber which any woodturner will know become part of one's life, were packed for removal.

Initially, they were stored in a warehouse while we house-hunted. I suppose it was then that they suffered their first rapid drying. In any event, they were no longer usable for large bowls, so I cut them up to make smaller bowls.

Now, with my new approach, they could, perhaps, be used again, if not full size, then at least larger than the bad cracking would normally allow.

ON THE SLAB

I had considered using my ruined slabs as barbecue wood, for each time I hauled out treasured pieces of jacaranda, plane or silky oak, I was devastated to see how badly they had cracked.

But pondering my friend's problem, it struck me those blocks might be usable after all. For she needed small, heavy bowls, which would be used outside, and so a rustic look would not be out of place.

With these thoughts in mind I took another look at my supplies.

I'd bought the timber from two suppliers in Natal, before leaving that province at the start of 1993. The 75mm 3″ and 100mm 4″ planks had been bandsawn into squares of roughly 300-400mm 11¾-15¾″, allowing them to dry on our

I inspected the blanks and chose those with the fewest and shallowest splits, preferring those where the larger surfaces were more or less free of deep cracks.

A few which had warped badly I discarded for possible later use, while on others I had to remove a section of the side or end.

I was left with some useful pieces to make heavy nut bowls, or what, in the spirit of naming for naming's sake, I thought I might now call *Emergent Bowls* or *Bowls in Becoming*. I managed to restrain myself from this, however — and from giving them numbers.

First, I cleaned up all the surfaces, mainly with a hand plane and belt sander. Each square or rectangular piece of wood was then screwed to a faceplate, or screw chuck.

I test-turned the block by hand to ensure it cleared the bed and the slide. The block was mounted bad side out and, after truing this up with a square

One of the slabs mounted, grooved and ready for further hollowing.

bottom and cutting the hollow, place the toolrest across the face of the block, **and keep hands on the far side of the toolrest.**

Also, use the slowest speed your lathe is geared down to. I know many woodturners understand these things. My warnings are for those who don't.

I realise that when you get to sanding the inside of the bowl, you have to disregard my second warning, but great care should be taken at all times.

One of the casuarina slab-bowls resting on the badly cracked section of stump from which it was cut.

The sharp edges of a spinning block can seriously damage unwary fingers.

On a recent batch, I resorted to slightly rounding the shoulders of the top of the bowl to lessen the chance of catching my fingers.

Back to work. Once the block has been securely mounted on the expanding collets, I again test turn it to ensure it turns freely before switching on the lathe.

With a pencil, held gently on the toolrest, I now inscribe a circle to tell me where the edge of the block is, so I know where the limits of the bowl should be.

I mark another circle about 5mm ³⁄₁₆″ in from this circle to indicate the inner wall of the

ended scraper, I removed it from the lathe and re-sanded the surface, keeping the faceplate in place.

Back on the lathe, I cut the recess for the biggest expanding collet. After this preparation, the block was reversed into the precision chuck and bowl hollowing began.

Some words of warning are necessary at this stage. There is a temptation to place rectangular pieces slightly off-centre to turn the hollow off-centre as well. I use a heavy lathe, well secured, and advise you to centre the block carefully, as any uneven weight can cause havoc with bearings.

Then, once the bowl has been mounted, both for cleaning the

Alec Jardine lived in Kloof, Natal, South Africa, and was a professor at the nearby University of Durban Westville, until he retired at the end of 1992 and moved to Port Elizabeth.

Seven years ago his doctor advised him to take up woodturning to take his mind off the stresses of a busy academic life.

He bought an old woodturning lathe and has been hooked ever since.

He has learned most of what he knows about woodturning from books, magazines, videos and "all manner of mishap, short of the disastrous."

Richard Raffan's earlier books and video helped channel his interest towards bowl turning, and he now spends most of his spare time turning out a variety of bowls.

He enjoys the challenge of turning some of the more difficult Southern

African woods, but rates plane and silky oak high on his list of favourite timbers.

Alec is fascinated by the unusual, and enjoys working with spalted wood, burls and parasitised woody growths. He has made a special study of spalting and has written extensively on the subject of fungal infection in timber.

He is married, and he and his wife have a grown-up family, who all support his hobby.

bowl. Using a square-ended scraper I carefully cut back the outer edges of the block up to the outer circle. I take it down about 10mm ³⁄₈″, so the circular bowl shape is in relief from the rest of the block. As I've said, I have recently taken to rounding off these shoulders.

The next step is to drill a depth guide hole. This I make half the diameter of the inner circle, if this isn't greater than

▶

the total depth of the wood.

Otherwise I use the total depth to guide me in my decision. I like to make the inside of these bowls as close to semi-spherical as possible.

Hollowing is done in the usual way, but I stress again, keep hands on the unbusy side of the toolrest. I use 10mm and 6mm bowl gouges for this, and work up to the inner circle.

To prevent skating back into the circumference I use the long corner of a skew chisel to score starter grooves in the wood.

I know that this is usual procedure for most bowl turners, but I stress it here, for skating back into the circumference could have dire consequences.

fingers — sanding. The spinning disc seems to exercise a hypnotic effect, and it's all too easy to become unaware of the outer edges.

I move the toolrest out of the way, but still keep both hands on the far side of an imaginary line drawn where it had been for the hollowing work, extending only the sandpapering hand beyond this point and into the bowl hollow.

I often apply a genérous quantity of sunflower seed oil to the inner bowl surface, allowing time for it to soak in. This makes sanding easier and less dusty and also darkens the wood, making the inner surface more obvious.

I work from about 80 grit down to about 360, and when

One block, whose sides displayed the saw marks of a large industrial bandsaw, I left rough after removal from the lathe. So it showed the progression from very rough sawing, through off-the-lathe roughness to the inner smoothness of the bowl hollow. It was well received and is, perhaps, the way to go. It certainly makes life a lot easier.

I make no claim to this being an original way of using timber. But it is a way of rescuing bits of timber and, I hope, will have given readers something to consider.

I realise the practice might be considered slightly dangerous, but it's safe enough if you heed advice. There are many other applications where the method could be used or adapted.

I have, for example, used up pieces from large logs of what I was told was tamarind, a dark, heavy wood with a reddish streak.

But it turned more like casuarina, and I'm inclined to believe this is what it was. The logs split and cracked dramatically while drying, making the wood impossible to use for normal bowl turning.

I was, however, able to rescue some interesting blanks, and used these with some of the bark still on one side.

I've also considered trying wedge-shaped pieces, both in the length and width, and seeing what results I can achieve, but that might only happen when I tire of the present novelty.

The turned bowls have been put to good use by my friend, who has requested something similar, but larger and shallower

'The next stage is fraught with danger — sanding. The spinning disc seems to exercise a hypnotic effect, and it's easy to become unaware of the outer edges.

I finish off with a heavy half round scraper I have ground to the required shape for bowl turning.

Having got this far, I examine the bowl carefully and decide whether I make the hollow wider or not. Usually I leave well alone, and then carefully, once more, work away at the outer edge of the bowl, using one or other of the bowl gouges to cut back to the flat edge of the block.

I usually work the bowl edge down to about 3-5mm wide, leaving an edge of flat wood about the same width at the closest edge.

This gives me space to cut into the flat section a little way, to suggest the bowl does not end at the flat surface. I use a sharp skew chisel for this. The depth of cut will depend on how much solid wood I have left at the closest edge to play with.

The next stage is fraught with danger for the hands and

satisfied with the finish, apply beeswax, rubbing down with a square of paper towel as the bowl spins.

The outer edge of the bowl poses special problems, and I usually resort to hand sanding the flat surface of the block as well as the outer edge of the bowl, once I have removed it from the lathe.

A section of completed slab bowls in silky oak, plane, Natal mahogany and casuarina.

for holding potato crisps.

Elsewhere the bowls have aroused interest and have also led to orders being placed for something similar. ■

Jim Kingshott, now aged 60, a craftsman of the old school and proud of it, started work in the woodworking industry at 14 years of age. He served a 5 years' apprenticeship as a cabinetmaker, which included woodturning.

For the past 11 years, as Apprentice Master at the Royal Aerospace Establishment in Farnborough, he has been responsible for teaching young woodworkers their craft.

With the help of his wife Jo, Jim also runs a small workshop making bespoke period furniture, which often has turned features incorporated into the design.

Jim says that woodworking is not just his way of life — it's his religion.

Beatrix Potter Table and Stools

JIM KINGSHOTT

A commission for a house made famous in a well-loved fairytale provides a project that will enchant young children everywhere.

In February 1980 I was asked by Frederick Warne & Co Ltd, who at the time were the publishers of the Beatrix Potter books (the copyright is now owned by Penguin), to design and make a small child's table and some stools for the newly-opened House of the Tailor of Gloucester, then as now the Beatrix Potter centre. The brief was that there should be seating for four children, aged three to five years, with a table of suitable height at which they could sit and look at the books.

I began by reading The Tailor of Gloucester. The illustrations showed mice sitting on cotton reels, so there was the very thing. What could be more fitting than giant-sized cotton reels, with a table stable enough to withstand youngsters climbing about on it.

The customer happened to visit the workshop just as I had finished making a flight of stairs from Parana pine. He was very taken with the colour of the wood and the smooth texture of the surface. It was probably the last wood I would have thought of using, but when questioned I could not find a reason good enough to turn it down. So that is how the job came to be made from Parana pine.

Now that I come to think about it, the wood in some ways is really quite suitable. Certainly its nice light colour is similar to those old wooden reels we enjoyed playing with as children before the advent of plastics. I'm sure the mice at the tailor's would not have sewn the waistcoat had there been only plastic stools for them to sit on.

The Tailor of Gloucester is the third tale in Beatrix Potter's Peter Rabbit series. It is based on something that actually occurred to a young Gloucester tailor, John S. Prichard, who was commissioned to make a coat for the city's mayor.

He returned to his workshop after a weekend break to find the finished clothes and a note saying No More Twist. Prichard believed it was the work of fairies, and advertised the fact in his shop window, but two colleagues later admitted to having returned to the shop and completing their employer's commission.

In the book it is a group of mice who complete the waistcoat, while the tailor is ill with fever, in repayment of his kind deed in rescuing them from his cat, Simpkin.

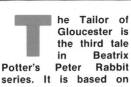

9, College Court, the House of the Tailor of Gloucester, is very much the house of the fictional tailor and is known as such to children all over the world.

The Stools

Making the stools and table can be very rewarding, especially if you have young children in the family. So, if you would like to have a go, here are the construction details.

Beginning with the cotton reel ends, cut out discs on the bandsaw and fix them to the outboard faceplate of your lathe. True up the ends to the correct diameter and work a half round on the circumference with a medium size deep gouge. This done, bore a 38mm 1½" hole through the centre of each end. This hole is important as, not only is it a dummy hole on the outside giving realism to the appearance, it also locates the inner disc onto which the core staves are assembled.

The inner disc is turned next, 210mm 8⅜" in diameter and 50mm 2" thick. Turn the outer part down to about 38mm 1½" thick, leaving a boss in the middle that is a good push fit in the hole of the end already turned.

Before taking the inner disc from the lathe mark a circle on its face at 200mm 8¹⁄₁₆" diameter. Space out 12 equal spaces around the perimeter and join the mark at the end of each space with a straight line. The line should just clip the circle marked at 200mm 8¹⁄₁₆" on the disc face.

The flats around the edge of the disc are worked to the lines just marked. There are several ways

of doing this — probably the easiest is on a disc sander. The flats can also be worked by laying the job down flat on a scrap piece of timber and paring vertically down with a chisel. If your paring is not up to this standard, a final touch with a plane can true the surface up, and should put things to right.

The staves are made up by planing a 15° bevel on both edges of a 65mm 2⅝" 22mm ⅞" board and cutting the ends square at 320mm 12½" length.

Fix the inner disc on the inside of the ends with six screws from the inside face. Glue and pin the staves into position between the ends, punch the pins well

down and leave the glue to set.

The outer surface of the staves is shaped up with a spoke shave and rasp, finally trueing up using a belt from a belt sander. OK, so you don't have one. Most tool shops sell replacement belts. A packet of three belts of 40 grit cost me £4.20 ($7.98) and, apart from the job in hand, they have many uses around the shop.

Make a cut across the belt so that you have a long strip of abrasive 100mm 4" or so wide and the full length of the belt. Fix the assembled reel so that the belt can be passed around the staves and, by gripping each end, is pulled backwards and forwards (like towelling your back after a shower), thus trueing up the outside surface of the staves.

After vacuuming away all the dust caused by the last process, the ends of the reels should be painted and the lettering applied. Then give the reels a coat of varnish before the cord,

which represents the cotton, is applied. This cord is sold by handicraft shops for weaving into tops for bedroom stools. Bore holes where the ends of the cord start and finish and glue and pin one end of the cord into a hole. Taking care to keep the cord tight, wind it round the reel making sure that each turn is close up against the previous one, and that it lies nice and flat. When the whole reel is covered, cut the cord and glue the end into its hole. It may be necessary to fix it with a little wooden peg driven into the hole with the cord.

That about finishes the reel but, as a final touch, I put three little rubber feet on the bottom end to make it stand firm on an uneven floor.

CUTTING LIST

Reel (For one off)

	No off	Length	Width	Thickness
Ends	2	305mm 12"	305mm 12"	32mm 1¼"
Inner Disc	2	230mm 9"	230mm 9"	50mm 2"
Staves	12	355mm 14"	63mm 2½"	25mm 1"

Table

Ply Top	1	560mm 22"	560mm 22"	12mm ½"
Lipping	6	510mm 20"	150mm 6"	38mm 1½"
Feet	2	840mm 33"	150mm 6"	50mm 2"
Bearers	2	840mm 33"	75mm 3"	32mm 1¼"
C/Post	1	760mm 30"	100mm 4"	100mm 4"

No more twist

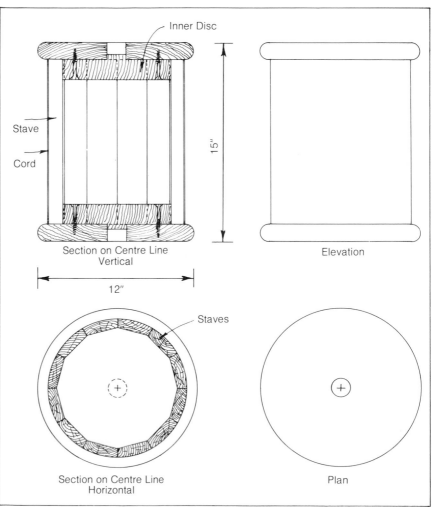

Beatrix Potter Cotton Reel

Inner Disc

Stave

Cord

15"

12"

Section on Centre Line Vertical

Elevation

Staves

Section on Centre Line Horizontal

Plan

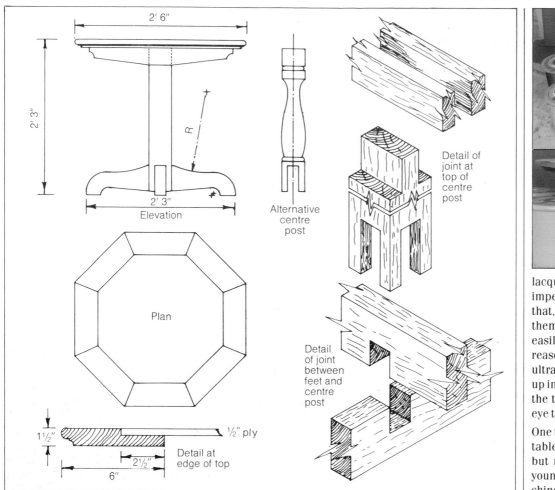

Elevation

Plan

Alternative centre post

Detail of joint at top of centre post

Detail of joint between feet and centre post

½" ply

Detail at edge of top

lacquer. The lacquer is impervious to most liquids so that, with small children using them, the table and reels can be easily kept clean. For some reason this lacquer reflects ultra-violet light which shows up in photographs as smears on the table top. But in fact to the eye there is just a shiny surface.

One thing is certain. Making the table and stools will do nothing but reflect to your credit. Any young boy or girl will take a shine to them on sight. ∎

The Table

The table is of very straight-forward construction; extra decoration can be added by turning the centre post instead of leaving it square, as on the original.

The feet are made from 150mm 6" x 50mm 2" halved together at the centre and cut to the profile on the drawing. 100mm 4" x 100mm 4" is used for the centre column, which is notched to fit down over the centre halving joint in the feet. At the top of the centre post a 75mm 3" x 32mm 1¼" notch is cut at each side to make a firm seating for the two top bearers. The bearers are bolted on either side with two 10mm ⅜" diameter coach bolts, passing through from one side to the other, sandwiching the tongue of the centre post between the bearers. These top bearers, cut from 75mm 3" x 32mm 1¼", are tapered in width from their full width at 50mm 2" either side of

the centre line to 45mm 1⅞" at the ends. The ends have a 25mm 1" radius quarter circle cut out of the lower outer corner as ornamentation.

The top is an 8-sided piece of 12mm ½" ply 305mm 1' to 255mm 10" across the flats with a lipping machined from 150mm 6" x 38mm 1½" mitred around it. The rebate in the lipping, into which the ply is fitted and well glued, makes quite a firm joint at the mitres. Even so I put a dowel in the outer half of each mitre. The hole for this dowel was jig bored on the Myford mortiseing attachment.

The top is fixed to the bearers using four stretcher plates. If you have not met these useful little chaps they are small lengths of angle about 38mm 1½" long with 20mm ¾" flanges. Each flange has a slot and a hole for screws.

The table and reels were finished with a clear Melamine

Beatrix Potter Table

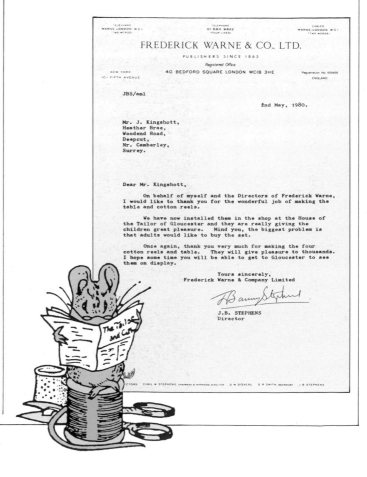

Simply Good for Salads

DAVE REGESTER

The first of a two-part article in which the author describes, in more detail than is normally the case, the making of a salad bowl.

Dave Regester became a woodturner, after working in a solicitor's office and going to University, because, he says, he realised he was happier making things with his hands than using his brain. He started turning full time in 1974 at a craft centre in Devon where he more or less taught himself.
Dave has always made a variety of items in locally available ash, burr oak and yew because he loves the grain. He makes salad bowls, scoops and platters, which he sells through high-class kitchen ware shops, and one-off pieces, which he sells through galleries and exhibitions.
Last year he had exhibitions at *Quercus*, Edinburgh, *The Ruskin Gallery*, Sheffield and *The Devon Guild of Craftsmen's* new headquarters in Bovey Tracy which holds regular exhibitions of members' work. In 1982 he was given a major award by South West Arts which helped him set up his own workshop in an old builder's yard, part of which is also his home.

A 254mm x 102mm 10″ x 4″ bowl with compound curve

Design and Preparing the Blank

There is no real practical reason for serving a salad in a wooden bowl. However, if you wish to add to the aesthetic appeal of the meal and enjoy the experience of handling a piece of smoothly turned wood, nothing can beat using a wooden bowl, especially if you have turned it yourself.

So, a salad bowl should look good on the table, but it should not be so stunning that it puts the salad in the shade. Take the bowl in photo A. You will see that the shape is simple but not uninteresting. It is not strictly a simple curve because that is an arc of a circle. If you were to make your bowl's profile exactly circular it would not satisfy your eye because that shape leads the eye to follow the curve and beyond.

The bowl in the photo has a compound curve. If you were to make a profile of one part of the curve, it would not match the next part. This looks good to me, probably because our eyes are more discerning than we tend to think. If there is sufficient interest in a shape to hold your attention, you are satisfied. If there is too much detail, you become satiated; and if there is too little variety of curve you get bored.

I know from personal experience that we tend to be so absorbed by the difficulties of making a bowl that design is relegated to the backburner. This explains why everyone, at the outset, produces a bowl with straight sides and a wide bottom, with a very abrupt curve at the bottom corner.

The only thing to be said for this shape is that it maximises the capacity. It not only looks boring but, even though you have not removed much wood from the outside, you have made a lot of work for yourself inside where it is more difficult to work. I am sure we have all had problems with that tricky sharp curve where the base meets the side.

If you can hold yourself back from the sensuous delights of shaving production for a moment and spend a little time with pencil and paper, you may find that what you produce gives you more than just the pleasure of having made something. You might actually make something worthy of a longer look.

Why not draw your blank from the side view (in other words a rectangle) and draw in a few profiles of possible bowls. It is cheaper and quicker than turning all those shapes. You will find some shapes more satisfying than others. If you make cardboard profiles of the shapes you like you can then see if they work as bowls.

It is surprisingly hard to master a simple shape but once you have done so, it is easy to reproduce with a flowing sweep of the gouge.

Too many people, I believe, are obsessed with bases. What marks there may be on the base are not relevant to function or appearance. If you wish to disguise the method you used to hold the bowl on to the lathe, that is up to you. Do not be bullied, by those who have learned to obliterate all evidence, into believing you must do the same. In some ways it is more honest to leave the screw holes visible (though tastefully filled) than to hide them. Never, in any event, be tempted to stick green baize on the base; it would not survive many washings.

Timber

Many timbers are suitable for salad bowls. Sycamore is the traditional one. It is easy to turn and stands up well to washing, though in common with many other woods it must not be allowed to remain damp. Ash and cherry are also suitable and

easily obtained from your local sawmill.

You can use dry timber for your bowl, if you can obtain it, but it will be expensive, especially if you have to buy it in small quantities. Savings may be made by buying in bulk, which is what some members of local chapters of the Association of Woodturners of Great Britain do. But even greater savings can be made by buying unseasoned timber in bulk and roughing out your bowls. Not only is wet timber cheaper than dry, it will have fewer cracks and will be easier to turn.

Here is how to rough out a salad bowl using wet timber. The tools you will need are as follows:

1 Lathe and faceplate

2 6mm ¼″ bowl gouge, 10mm ⅜″ bowl gouge, 6mm ¼″ depth gouge, 32mm 1¼″ domed scraper and 12mm ½″ square ended scraper (see photo B).

B Gouges and scrapers

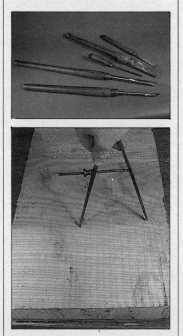

C Marking the circle

3 Calipers, rulers, screw driver, finishing paper (60, 80, 100, 180 and 220 grit), vegetable oil and wax.

4 Benchgrinder

Your bowl awaits you in the plank; it is now up to you to liberate it. Before cutting the plank, examine it carefully for defects. Look on both faces for cracks, knots and bark intrusions. There will be some

cracks on the end of the plank, however wet the wood, because it will have dried before being planked. It is a good idea, if you are unsure of the depth to which the cracks penetrate, to cut slices off the end of the plank with a chainsaw until there are no cracks left.

The bowl in the photo is 250mm x 100mm 10″ x 4″. So to allow for shrinkage you should set your calipers to describe a circle 275mm 10¾″ diameter. Mark a circle on the wood and leave a clear dent in the centre so you can locate it again (see photo C).

Detach the blank from the plank using a chainsaw. If you do not have a bandsaw, use the chainsaw also to trim the blank to a fairly circular shape. I recommend a chainsaw, if you do not already possess a bandsaw, because they are cheaper to buy and easy to hire for occasional use. Do be careful with them **and always use the correct safety gear which you should be able to hire with the saw**.

Look carefully at the blank and decide which face you would like to be the top of the bowl. Look first for defects in the timber that you may be able to turn off. For instance, there may be a knot in the centre of the blank which you will be able to lose if you make that the inside of the bowl.

If you do not mind screw holes in the base of your bowl, there is no reason why you should not screw your faceplate to the blank and rough it out in one operation. You must make sure you locate two of the screw holes in a line parallel with the grain because, when the bowl dries, the wood will shrink less along the grain than across it. You will need to remount the blank, using these holes, when it has dried. I have made many hundreds of bowls in one operation, using just two screws. But if you are not very experienced, you may prefer to use four screws while roughing out and then only two for the subsequent re-turning.

If you wish to turn a bowl with no sign of how you attached the wood to the lathe, you could leave a foot on the bowl and remove it when you have finished, losing the screw holes in the foot. This is rather

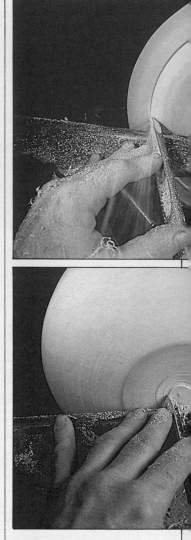

D Making the first cut with a 10mm ⅜″ gouge

E Deflecting the shavings

wasteful and will work out expensive if you make many bowls.

I shall describe a method, using the precision combination chuck supplied by Craft Supplies and the Axminster Power Tools' four jaw chuck, which is the most efficient method I have found for making a bowl from wet wood leaving no mounting marks.

Once you have worked out which face of your blank is to be the base you must ascertain the centre of the other face . . . unless this is the face on which you originally marked out the blank. You can forget all the complicated methods you may have read using arcs of circles and log. tables. All you need to do is stick your calipers where

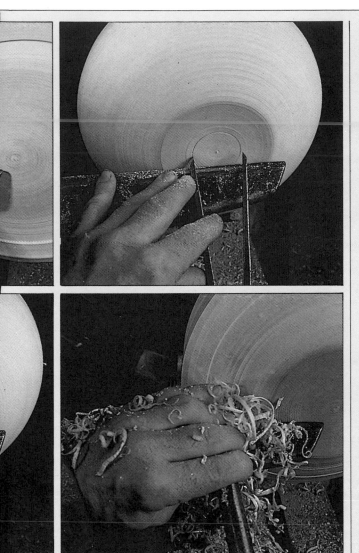

are cutting are supported by the fibres on the other side of them. The gouges I use are made of high-speed steel because they keep their edge longer than carbon steel. As you will see from the photo, I grind the bevel right back as this makes the tool more versatile.

The tool is held on its side, with the open part of the flute pointing away from the work, cutting with the part of the edge that is just below the point. As with most tools, you start off with the part of the tool where the bevel meets the body of the tool rubbing on the work. This does not cut any shavings but you then slowly move the end of the tool handle, with your hand which is not on the tool rest, using the fingers of your hand on the rest as fulcrum, so that the edge of the tool bites into the wood. At this moment you must start your sweeping cut.

Never stop with the tool still in contact with the wood as this is likely to result in a catch or at least a mark on the work.

Get into the habit of doing cuts in sweeping arcs and end a cut by raising the cutting edge off the work and carrying through away from the work. If you work in sweeping arcs you will produce smooth curves which are easy to finish smoothly. If you make tentative jabs, your work will have many grooves in it which are remarkably difficult to remove.

Space does not allow me to go into the intricacies of tool sharpening here. Suffice it to say it is vital your tools are sharp at all times and that your bevels are concave.

The grip you use to hold the tool onto the rest will vary with your manual dexterity and personal preference. My grip is unusual and would not suit everyone. But it does mean I have a sensitivity of control over the tool which enables me to respond to slight changes in the textures of the wood which those with more firm grips on the tool may not be able to do. In any case there is no need to hold onto the tool so that your knuckles whiten. You are then in no position to respond to the wood.

The same principle applies to your grip on the end of the handle. As with all hand tools,

both hands work together to put the edge to the work so that it cuts the wood. The motive power is provided by the lathe. If you are having to push hard you are doing something wrong. Either the tool is not sharp or you are using the wrong part of the edge, or you are holding the tool at the wrong angle.

When something is going wrong, change some aspect of what you are doing. Do not keep flogging away or you will dishearten yourself.

As you progress you will learn to hold the tool so that, not only do you cut efficiently, but you can also (as in photo E) deflect the shavings away from your face.

The first cuts on the outside of the bowl should start with the tool rest parallel to the base of the bowl and as close to it as possible. It should be below the centre so that the tool is pointing upwards. The exact height will depend on your own height and the angle at which you hold the tool.

As you remove more wood, stop the lathe and move the rest around the outside of the bowl so that the tool is supported as close to the lathe as possible. This is to prevent the tool chattering, a result of the shaft flexing between tool rest and cutting edge.

The base of the bowl has to be wider than the chuck and I suggest 90mm 3½″ to 100mm 4″. A small base makes the bowl float on the table and should give you no problems with stability unless you go too far. The part in between the base and lip is where you have to make your decisions as to shape. But since you are roughing out the bowl, there is some margin for error as long as you are not too far from the final shape you require. You will be able to look at the bowl while it is drying and think about the final shape at your leisure.

When the outside of the bowl is roughed out, make a recess on the base to fit your chuck. Make the base flat using the 10mm ⅜″ gouge's long edge and, working from the centre outwards, leaving a slight hollow in the base to ensure it will stand firmly. With your calipers set at the size of the chuck inserts (in this case 70mm 2¾″), mark the base using just one of the points (photo F).

you think the centre is and try to describe a circle. If this does not coincide with the outside of the blank, move the calipers about until it does and then push the centre point in to make a definite mark at the centre.

F Marking the base

G Hollowing out the recess

mark the places for the screws with a bradawl. Then just whack the bradawl and you should be able to drive home the screws

---

'I have covered a lot of ground that is basic to turning, leaving out none of the little wrinkles I have learnt from other people and my own experience.'

If you have a single screw chuck that is strong enough, you can use this to mark the blank. If not, you must use a faceplate, which takes a little longer. To mark the screw holes I use a circle of hardboard, the same size as the faceplate, with holes in it corresponding to the screw holes and the centre. You simply place the circle over the centre mark on the blank and

without further ado.

The speed you turn the bowl is up to you. My only advice is that you should start at a slow speed and work up to what you find comfortable and safe.

The first cut should be made with the 10mm ⅜″ gouge, with the rest across the base, cutting from the base towards the lathe (see photo D). This is cutting downhill so that the fibres you

H Finishing off the edge of the recess

I Measuring the required depth

J Levelling off the face of the bowl

K Letting the tool do the cutting

6mm ¼″ Dowel

⁵⁄₈″ 15mm

⁵⁄₈″ 15mm

15mm

A simple depth gauge

Hollow out the recess using a 6mm ¼″ gouge (photo G) and finish off the edge of the recess using a 12mm ½″ scraper (photo H). This tool is ground on the skew so that it produces the angle of cut to match the angle of the inserts. The depth of recess need not be as deep as the insert. But until you are proficient you should make it about 6mm ¼″ deep to ensure your bowl is firmly gripped.

Before you remove the bowl from the lathe, it is a good idea to check that the chuck fits the recess.

Remove the work from the lathe, take off the faceplate and then screw the combination chuck onto the lathe. Now is a good time to measure the depth of the bowl by standing it on a flat surface and holding a ruler against the side. I usually forget until it is on the lathe at which stage you have to hold one ruler across the base and another at right angles to it from the lip.

(To overcome this problem, why not make a simple depth gauge. You can construct one in moments from a suitable length of hardwood drilled in the centre to accept a length of dowel with a fairly tight fit. You will find it useful to have a choice of several such gauges. — Ed)

Now the bowl is offered up to the chuck which is gripped.

Turn the work by hand to check that it is concentric and not fouling the rest which is set the front of the work. If the bowl is to be approximately 250mm 10″ across, the aim should be to across make the wall thickness approximately 25mm 1″ all round. An even wall thickness will promote drying and 25mm 1″ should give you sufficient thickness to turn off bulges caused by warping and any small surface cracks that may occur during drying.

You must therefore deduct 25mm 1″ from the depth of the bowl to give you the inside depth. To ensure you do not go too deep while hollowing out, drill a hole in the blank to the depth required. I do this with a

6mm ¼″ gouge ground straight across with the bevel at 30° from the flat of the tool. I measure the required depth on the tool as in photo I and make a small cone-shaped opening in the centre. Then I push the tool in, holding it with the hand being used to measure the depth. Do not press too hard, and pull the tool out frequently to clean off the swarf. On no account leave go of the tool unless it is jammed in so firmly that your hand is burning. In this event step back smartly in case the tool flies out and stop the lathe before trying to extricate it.

The beauty of roughing out a number of bowls is that you can experiment with your tool technique without worrying about finishing. You are also cutting the wood when it is in the best condition to do so — when it is wet.

Start the hollowing process by levelling off the face of the bowl (see photo J) then enlarge the hole in the middle so that you end up with a shallow cone extending to the rim, which of course will be 25mm 1″ thick. If you wish to mark this thickness with a 12mm ½″ scraper this will also give you a stop to prevent your gouge skating off the edge of the bowl. You should soon reach the stage where you are sufficiently familiar with the angle at which you hold the gouge for this not to be necessary.

It really is the most satisfying feeling to whack out the centre of a bowl in about five minutes. In fact it seems to take longer to clear up the shavings than it does to do the turning! It is best to speed up slowly, however. Do not force the pace and always let the tool do the cutting (photo K).

When the little dot that your depth gouge has left in the centre finally disappears you have gone far enough. You should then check with the calipers that you have an even wall thickness. Perfect accuracy is not essential at this stage and with experience you should be able to do this by feel. ■

The second part of this article (see next page) describes how to dry roughed out bowls and then re-turn them.

Bowls that have been roughed out of wet timber must be dried out as evenly as possible. When water is evaporated into air the temperature of the air is lowered and as we all know, cold air falls. Imagine, then, a downward flow of air over a drying bowl. To ensure the air passes down without interruption, we must prevent it from gathering in the bowls. This is best done by inverting the bowl, on a rack of 25mm 1″ slats with a 25mm 1″ gap, in a place where there is a steady circulation of air and which rain cannot penetrate.

Happy Returns

In the right conditions, the bowl should dry within a few months. If you record on the bowl the weight and date when you roughed it out, you will be able to weigh it at regular intervals. When the weight has stabilised it is as dry as it will get in those conditions. Bowls re-turned after such a drying process are more stable than bowls turned from dry wood in one go. This is because, in taking out the middle, you release the tensions in the wood that cause some of the warping.

Roughed out bowls may crack if the grain is particularly wild or if the drying process is speeded up either by hot dry weather or by artificial means, such as putting the work in an enclosed space with a source of heat or a de-humidifier. I have used a domestic de-humidifier for a number of years now to dry bowls in bulk, a process that can be accomplished in a month. Cracking is prevented by covering the end grain with any substance that will stop the water evaporating too quickly. You may use paint, but beware as this can penetrate certain woods. You may also use glue or heated wax but the cheapest and most convenient substance is emulsified paraffin wax, particularly if you buy it in bulk.

Photo L shows the shelves in my workshop where I keep my dried-out bowls. The photograph was taken after Christmas when stocks were a little low. Nonetheless you can see that even with depleted stocks you can respond to an order much faster than you can turning from the solid.

L Dried-out bowls

Simply Good for Salads

DAVE REGESTER

In this final part of his article the author describes how to dry roughed out bowls and then re-turn them.

Dave Regester has been turning professionally since 1974. In his workshop in Tiverton, Devon, he makes salad bowls, scoops and platters, which he sells through high-class kitchenware shops, and one-off pieces, which he sells through galleries and exhibitions.

When a bowl has dried out and you are ready to re-turn it, it must be remounted on the lathe. If you used a faceplate when roughing it out, you should be able to remount it using the same screw holes. The bottom probably will not be flat but you can plane it so that the faceplate sits firmly.

If you elected to use a Combination chuck, you may find the recess has not warped too much to prevent you using the chuck without more ado. If however the recess has warped too much you will have to remount the bowl so that the recess can be trued up.

The most flexible method I have found for doing this is to use the 4-jaw chuck made by Axminster Power Tools. They provide a set of jaws to which you can attach quadrants of wood. These can be turned to accept all possible bowl sizes as in photos M and N.

A less efficient method is seen in photo O. This is a roughed-out bowl but you could also use any piece of wood of the right size. All you do is turn a recess in the wood to accept the bowl but it must be tapered and, because it is no longer circular, glue must be used to attach the bowl where its sides do not touch the wood. Hot glue is best for this purpose.

Once you have trued up the base of the bowl, and the

M & N Remounting the bowl ↓

O A less efficient method ↑

recess, you must check to see that the Combination chuck will still expand to fit. There is a good amount of expansion in this chuck but, should you find that you have exceeded this, you will either have to use the next size up or turn off the recess altogether and turn a new one of the correct size.

If you do not mind the recess in the base of the finished bowl, you may now sand the base. Do be careful not to sand the edge of the recess as this will make it asymmetrical and it will no longer grip so well.

You are now in a position to mount the bowl in the chuck and re-turn it. First job is to true up the top edge (photo P) and then the outside (photo Q). As

P Trueing up the top edge ↓

Q Re-turning the outside ↓

You can see that the finish is better after this cut. A skew scraper can be used in the same way.

A professional has to consider whether he is using the quickest means to achieve the required result: it is a nice point whether you achieve a good finish by tool or finishing paper. You must certainly get rid of all major blemishes with the tool because it is more time-consuming and costly to use finishing paper. If you rely overmuch on sanding, you end up with a bowl that does not have a true surface. You should inspect the surface carefully before you proceed to sand because, if you sand and then see a bad flaw which you need to use the tool to remove, you will find that small pieces of grit will have embedded themselves in the wood and these will blunt the tool.

When you re-turn the inside, you may need to start yourself off by making a cut into the solid wood at the rim with the 6mm ¼" scraper so that you have a firm edge to rest the bevel or the gouge on. Aim for an even wall thickness when you finish the inside. This will ensure that the weight of the bowl will feel right when it is picked up. Whether this is 12mm ½" or 10mm ⅜" or whatever is a matter of personal

S Using the 6mm ¼" gouge

R Making a very fine cut

you will see, this is done with the tool working from the base towards the lip (downhill of the grain). The outstanding parts are obviously removed first. These are most extreme at the lip and, as the wood rotates, it will appear to be transparent at this point. You should present your tool to the work as though the outside of this blur is solid wood and not take off very thick shavings until the outside of the bowl is circular.

Final Shape

Now you can decide on the final shape. Looking at the profile of the work (not the tool) will enable you to see the shape, and sweeping cuts from the base right up to the lip should enable you to make a smooth curve. When you think you have got a good shape, remove the bowl from the lathe and look at it as if it were on a table.

You will find the direction of the light makes it look quite different in this position and you may decide to alter the shape accordingly. This is the point where your decision will make the difference between a good bowl and one that is not so good.

While making sure that the shape is right you will probably have been taking off quite small shavings. This should mean that the surface of the bowl does not have too many ridges or torn fibres. At this point I like to sharpen my 10mm ⅜" gouge and make a very fine cut using the long side of the tool and working towards the base from the top (photo R). You must

keep the bevel close to the work for this cut to succeed and apply very little pressure, otherwise you will have an almighty catch. As you will see from the photo, this tool can produce a fairly smooth finish. It can be improved by applying some oil (compatible with the finish) to the surface, particularly on the end grain, and then using the 6mm ¼" gouge as in photo S.

preference. It should not be too thick, however, as whoever serves the salad has to be able to pick up the bowl!

Again the bulk of the material is removed using the 10mm ³/₈″ gouge. When you are satisfied that the bowl has an even wall thickness, you can proceed to use the 6mm ¼″ gouge to get a smooth surface inside (see photo T).

Finally, use the tool fresh from the grinder, after applying oil, as you did on the outside. I often do a fine sweep with the 38mm 1¼″ scraper to get rid of the very last fluffy bits, but do keep feeling the inside to make sure the shape is correct.

finish off with hand-held 220 grit to get rid of the last traces of sanding marks.

The finish you put on a salad bowl must be tasteless, non-toxic and odourless. It must also respond well to frequent washing. For these reasons, I use a cheap vegetable cooking oil wiped on with a cloth. I then rub a piece of beeswax over the surface, while the work is turning, and use the motion of the lathe to buff it with a cloth. This makes the bowl feel nice but the wax soon washes off.

Maintaining the finish is simplicity itself. All you need do is wash the bowl and, when it looks a bit dull, rub some more

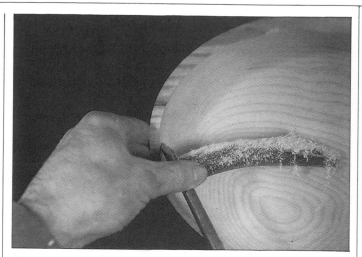

T Smoothing the inside

'I have covered a lot of ground that is basic to turning, leaving out none of the little wrinkles I have learnt from other people and my own experience.'

Finishing

The finish inside and out can be done with hand-held finishing paper, preferably a full sheet cut into four and each quarter folded over three times to protect you from the heat generated by friction. Start with paper as coarse as you need and only when you have removed all imperfections proceed to the next grade. Many turners now use power sanding as this is much quicker and saves sore fingers. The velcro system supplied by Craft Supplies is very good but I recommend that you keep one pad for each grade and change over the pad rather than the disc as this reduces the life of the velcro before the grit loses its edge.

It is quite easy to develop the knack of removing one pad from the drill with a flick of the wrist and tightening up the next one using the force of the motor against the pressure of your hand on the chuck. You will see from photo U the sort of angle at which to hold the drill. Some experimentation will be necessary to work out the best angle for you. You will soon learn that it is vital for the direction of the pad to be opposite that of the work!

I use the 60, 120 and 180 grit pads unless I am doing really well, in which case I miss out the first of these. But I like to

oil on. The oil in French dressing is the same as the finishing oil. So, after a few years, the bowl will develop a superb patina which is better than any finish you can apply.

The bowl is now finished, if you do not mind leaving the chucking recess. If you want to get rid of this, you must remount the bowl. The Axminster chuck is ideal for this but you must protect the top edge of the bowl with a piece of cloth so that the wooden jaws do not leave any

marks. If you do not have this chuck, you may use a wooden blank or roughed out bowl again. But you will not have to use glue to keep it in place as it will be perfectly circular.

If you simply used a faceplate throughout, you can remount the bowl, to give the base a good finish, and then fill the screw holes with a mixture of Super Glue or Araldite and some

U The drill angle

sanding dust. Super Glue dries almost instantaneously with most woods but, in the case of others, may not. In which case a burst of Craft Supplies' 'Hot Shot' will make it do so.

The best reason for not using a faceplate is that it reduces the amount of chemicals you need to use.

Now all you have to do is wash your salad or sell your bowl. You are on your own. ∎

The completed bowl. 254mm 10″ x 102mm 4″

TURN A DROP SPINDLE

Photo 1 Rough body and shaft with collet for fitting in the chuck.

ERNIE CONOVER

Ernie spins a yarn and shows how to get you and your partner weaving.

Ernie Conover is our contributing editor in America. He teaches woodworking in general, and woodturning in particular, at Conover Workshops, a school he and his wife Susan operate together. In addition to writing and lecturing widely, he is a technical consultant to a number of companies on design and manufacture of woodworking tools and machines.

'While not everyone is ambitious enough to make a spinning wheel, a drop spindle is within the ability of even the neophyte turner. In fact, it is a very good learning exercise.'

I have received much positive feedback from all the project articles I have written for **Woodturning**. Readers constantly ask for more. Talking to fellow woodworkers over the years, I have come to the conclusion that there is a significant overlap between woodworkers and their spouses who are interested in spinning and/or weaving. So I offer this project that should be of interest to a significant number of readers. It also makes a good craft project that sells well at craft shows.

Both my mother and my wife, Susan, are spinners and weavers. Some of my earliest childhood remembrances are of watching my mother weave, so at an early age I knew warp from weft. It is only natural that I have turned my woodworking talents, at times, to making and repairing weaving equipment. While not everyone is ambitious enough to make a spinning wheel, a drop spindle is within the ability of even the neophyte turner. In fact, it is a very good learning exercise.

A drop spindle is a spinning wheel in its simplest form — sort of a pole lathe spinning wheel. Like the pole lathe, the drop spindle has been used from time immemorial to make useful articles for daily use and is still used in remote areas today.

The neophyte spinner will find it instructive to first use the drop spindle before moving on to a true spinning wheel, and children will find it just plain fun. Any conclave of spinners will find one or two spinning on drop spindles just to add variety, and maybe a bit of bravado, to the occasion.

Some readers may have a friend or loved one who is only tentative about their desire to take up spinning. To launch would-be spinners on their way, Susan helped me to write the *Directions For Using a Drop Spindle*. This separate piece, combined with a pleasurable hour or so in the workshop, will provide the perfect gift for your would-be spinner. It may even start a new hobby that will bring a lifetime of pleasure to you and your friend.

A drop spindle is nothing more than a giant top that spins suspended on a thread rather than on its point. The central shaft is made from a 305mm 12" length of dowel. I use standard ▶

8mm ⁵⁄₁₆″ hardware dowel for the project, but zealots may wish to turn the dowel as well.

The body of the drop spindle is made from a 25mm 1″ thick x 85mm 3¼″ DIA disc of any suitable hardwood. This is another beauty of this project — it can be made from scraps.

I like cherry, but any sound piece of timber will do. Since the body provides a reservoir of energy, storing the energy of each spin, some weight is an advantage, so overly light woods should be avoided.

Cut out 85mm 3¼″ circles of the chosen 25mm 1″ timber with a band saw or coping saw. Drill a 8mm ⁵⁄₁₆″ hole at the centre mark left by the compass or dividers. This hole should be square to the surface and a press fit with the dowel. A pillar drill (drill press) is best but the job can be done adequately with a bit brace or portable electric drill. Since wood drills often tend to drill slightly oversize, I use a ¹⁹⁄₆₄″ metal twist drill which is ¹⁄₆₄″ under the dowel size.

You can also drill the blank in the lathe (see my article in Issue 9 of **Woodturning**) in which case the lathe becomes a pillar drill on its side. Mount the drill bit in a drill chuck mounted in the spindle and place the work on a drill pad in the tailstock.

If you are using a hand-held drill, a brad point drill bit will give you a cleaner and more accurate hole than an ordinary twist drill.

Glue the freshly-drilled disc so about 25mm 1″ of dowel protrudes and set it aside to dry while you build the chuck. Turning small production items in one of the many available metal chucks is appealing. The trouble is that three or four jaw universal chucks leave marks, and spigot chucks will not hold small diameters like our 8mm ⁵⁄₁₆″ shaft.

Fortunately there is an easy way to modify most metal chucks to hold the drop spindle securely without leaving marks.

That is to turn a wood collet that will fit into the metal chuck and hold the shaft of the drop spindle. In this way the metal chuck really acts as a collet closer, supplying the force necessary to close the jaws of the collet.

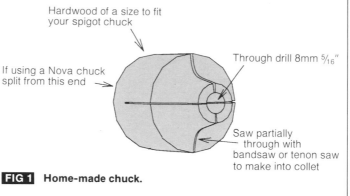

Hardwood of a size to fit your spigot chuck

If using a Nova chuck split from this end →

Through drill 8mm ⁵⁄₁₆″

Saw partially through with bandsaw or tenon saw to make into collet

FIG 1   Home-made chuck.

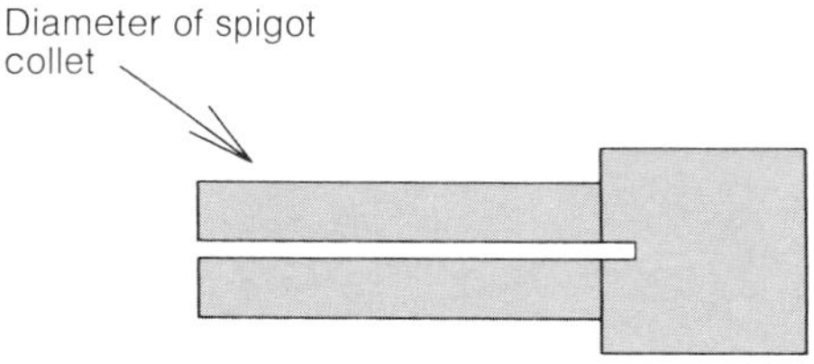

Diameter of spigot collet

FIG 2   If using a spigot chuck this design may work better.

As you can see from my sketch (FIGS 1 and 2), making the collet is simple. It is initially turned between centres to the desired outside diameter. Outside diameter will depend on the metal chuck you own. The collet has to have sufficient diameter to have some strength once centre drilled 8mm ⁵⁄₁₆″. If using a spigot chuck I would pick the largest jaws you possess for it, but a minimum of 20mm ¾″ is necessary.

I used a small four-jaw universal Nova chuck which is designed especially for woodturning. Being four jaw it will grip squares well, and has a variety of accessories which screw to dovetailed slots in the jaws with socket head machine screws. I have sketched my collet for the Nova chuck. It is 50mm 2″ DIA at the big end and tapers down to 35mm 1⅜″ over its 45mm 1¾″ length.

Drilling the collet should be done with it held in your chuck and should be on exact centre. By cutting a dimple at the centre with a small spindle gouge it is easy to start the drill on exact centre. Drill for a slide fit with the dowel.

Now split the chuck into four fingers by partially sawing through it. While the job can be done effectively in a bandsaw, some danger is present when cutting rounds. It is best to cradle the round in a wood V block during cutting so it cannot roll. The safest way to slit the collet is with a tenon saw. If you are using a Nova chuck you will have to slit from the opposite end from that shown in my drawing. I have drawn the design for using a closing ring.

As an aside, here is an important safety point for all jaw-type chucks. Never work

Photo 2 Starting shaping the body.

Photo 3 Shaping the reverse side.

Photo 4 Rounding the bottom end of the shaft (nubbin).

with any jaw more than half way out of the body of the chuck. I would even say no more than 40% of the jaw which leaves 60% safely inside the body and held by the scroll.

Hyperextending the jaws is an invitation for one or more jaws not to be engaged by the scroll (which is a spiral thread that actuates the jaws). Alternately the end of the scoll can snap off because it barely engages one jaw. Either situation allows one or more jaws to go ballistic when you start the lathe.

If you do not own a metal chuck of any sort there is still a way. By increasing my basic design to 90mm 3½″ DIA it can be screwed to a faceplate. When screwing into end grain in this way use sheet metal screws as they will hold better.

Now by turning a gentle taper on the nose the chuck may be closed by forcing a ring over it. Often a suitable ring can be found around the house or workshop, but if not the ring may be turned as well. By simply tapping the ring down over the taper with a small hammer the chuck is closed.

In this case the work will have to be reversed in the chuck to reach the top side, but that is easy because the collet grips with perfect concentricity. In most cases a home-made

Photo 5 Applying the finish.

Photo 7 Applying some carnauba wax before final burnishing.

Photo 6 Burnishing with shavings.

Photo 8 The piece is reversed so the shaft can be sanded.

Photo 9 The finished body.

collet chuck is better than one used in a metal chuck as the closer, and is much cheaper.

The actual turning of the drop spindle is quite simple (Photos 1-4). Grip the long end of the shaft with the wood disc butted up against the face of the chuck. A turning speed between 1100 RPM and 1700 RPM will do the job nicely.

A small bowl gouge is the right tool for the job, or lacking that a small round nose scraper. A spindle gouge is the wrong tool because any catch will result in a broken shaft.

Since this is pure faceplate turning you must work from smaller diameters to larger diameters to lay grain down. This is just the opposite from spindle turning. Shape to my drawing of the drop spindle.

If you are using a home-made ring closing chuck you will have to turn the project by halves. When the long end of the dowel is exposed it is useful to bring the tailstock spindle up so that the end of the dowel is inside it. This will keep it from whipping around wildly.

Of course you can turn the body shape first and then drill the centre hole and glue in the shaft afterwards, but with that method the drop spindles often turn out unbalanced.

It is difficult to hold the body alone with a metal chuck for

turning without leaving marks. It can be done with a home-built screw chuck but screw chucked parts are seldom concentric with the axis of the centre hole or from side to side.

My chucking method grabs the shaft so the body can be turned concentric with it. It gives a perfect part, as if it were turned from one piece.

I finally shape the dowel in the lathe. Turn the radius on the long end by placing the work against your hand and using a small spindle gouge or coarse sandpaper. Saw the notch with a coping or jigsaw and plane or sand a tapered flat about 50mm 2" long on one side (FIG 3).

I sand my drop spindles to 220 grit and apply a French polish. I apply a 2½ pound cut of orange shellac while the work is still in the lathe (Photo 5). I then start the lathe at 1700 RPM and burnish the shellac with shavings from the floor (Photo 6), then crayon on some pure carnauba wax and re-burnish with shavings (Photo 7). The result is a beautiful finish that will last.

I also sand and finish the shaft by reversing in the chuck (Photo 8). You do not want rough wood that yarn will catch on. The French polish and wax provides a perfect surface that is smooth and nonstaining to the yarn (Photo 9).

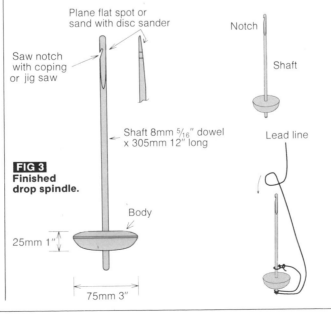

Plane flat spot or sand with disc sander

Saw notch with coping or jig saw

Shaft 8mm ⁵/₁₆" dowel x 305mm 12" long

FIG 3
Finished drop spindle.

Body

25mm 1"

75mm 3"

Notch

Shaft

Lead line

Directions For Using a Drop Spindle (A wild and woolly yarn by Ernie and Susan Conover)

1) Tie off a lead line to the shaft with two half hitches. Pass it around the fly wheel and twice around the nubbin. Bring it back around the flywheel and secure it to the notch by making an underhand loop. The lead line should end about 150mm 6" to 200mm 8" above the notch.

2) Tear away a small wisp of wool and twist it to the lead line.

3) Hold your wool in your left hand and with your right start the drop spindle spinning in a clockwise direction. The short length of wool you started with will be spun into thread. As this happens tear away some more — about 50mm 2". Re-spin the drop spindle as often as need be.

Susan Conover using the drop spindle.

Your left hand should hold the wool and your right should be about 50mm 2" below, controlling how much the thread is twisted by the pressure of your fingers. If your wool breaks away, fear not — simply tear a bit away and rejoin it to your previous work by twisting together.

4) Continue until the drop spindle almost touches the floor. Now pinch off the thread with your left hand and wrap it once around your left index finger. Undo the lead line (subsequently the thread itself) from the notch and wrap it around the shaft. Do this by holding the nubbin against your hip and spinning the drop spindle clockwise with your right hand. Feed the thread onto the shaft with your right.

5) Leaving about 50mm 2" free, re-secure the thread to the notch with one underhand loop. Continue the process until you have sufficient thread for your needs. ■

Ron Kent lives and works in Honolulu, Hawaii. He is famous as a turner of beautiful translucent bowls made from Norfolk pine which are in private, corporate and institutional collections worldwide.

But Ron, who is 61 and married with two grown-up children, is a man of many parts. He is a graduate engineer, a veteran stockbroker of 30 years, an adult education teacher and call-in radio talk-show host on personal finance and investment, and a conductor of seminars on finance and creativity.

Despite all this he still manages to spend some 15 hours a week at woodturning and sculpture, and he admits he enjoys being well paid for doing the things he loves.

His work has been featured in several previous issues of *Woodturning*.

Have you ever had a special block of wood, precious to you because of its beauty, its uniqueness, or possibly because of how it came into your possession?

You would like to enrich and enhance its beauty by turning it into a special bowl — but you are loath to risk failure. I know, I've been there.

A few years ago, I solved the problem to my own complete satisfaction by turning the blocks into ovoid forms about 100mm 4″ maximum DIA by maybe 150mm 6″ long — about the size and shape of an ostrich egg.

Let me tell you something about eggs: they are almost mystical in their appeal. Here is how I learned about eggs nearly 12 years ago. Much of my lathe work in those days consisted of the bottle/decanter form, experimenting with various aesthetically pleasing silhouettes.

One of my favourite designs was an elliptical body with thin neck leading to a flared lip. One day it occurred to me to eliminate the neck and lip entirely, and to round the bottom — you guessed it, an egg.

I liked that one so much I brought it into the house that night and kept it on my nightstand, then took it to work the next morning.

The effect of large wooden eggs on other people is a lesson

RON KENT

A look at two turners with a fascination for turned wooden eggs, and how they make them. In this first article, Ron Kent discusses: How I lathe an egg — and why.

epitome of aesthetic perfection.

And there are more 'sensible' people whose logical minds reject such intuitive frippery. Their *logic* rejects it, but their souls still feel the tug. You can recognise these people by their obvious emotional discomfort, often manifest in ridiculous jokes ("Are you going to sit on this to hatch it?"), or exaggerated rejection ("Stupid!").

There also are those to whom this whole thing is a mystery. "Wooden eggs? So what? Who cares?"

But enough psychology! Let's get back to craft.

Most of my own turning is done with logs rather than lumber — sometimes seasoned,

yourself by intimidated by those freaks whose every cut is clean perfection. Sandpaper is *good*, and is good for you.

Here's how I turn an egg. I start with a section of tree trunk (in this case Norfolk pine) 200mm-300mm 8″-12″ long by 150mm-200mm 6″-8″ DIA. This is mounted between centres along the linear axis of the grain (Photo 1). I use a large spur

Photo 1 Rough log mounted between centres.

driving centre in the headstock and a ball bearing centre in the tailstock.

Before cutting the log I take account of where the knots are. I try to ensure that these will be near the broadest diameter of the egg.

The rough log is turned to a smooth cylinder with flat ends (Photos 2 and 3). For this job I use a broad blade scraper and undercut to make a planing cut rather than scrape. ▶

> '**The effect of large wooden eggs on other people is a lesson in Freudian psychology . . . you'd be amazed at individual responses.**'

in Freudian psychology. I keep an egg on the desk in my office and display others for sale in galleries and craft fairs. You'd be amazed at individual responses.

There are people (like myself) to whom this shape is irresistible. We see it as the

often green, usually somewhere in between. I always work between centres, most often with the linear axis of the tree comprising the major (longer) axis of my egg.

My tools of choice are gouge, broad-blade scraper, and, of course, sandpaper. Don't let

TO WORK ON
AN EGG

Aromatic cedar.

Photo 2 Part smoothed to a cylinder.

Photo 3 The cylinder is trued.

Starting with the lathe at moderate speed (about 800 RPM), you can increase to 1200 RPM when the cylinder is true.

Next I start the shaping. I begin at the area of maximum diameter and cut towards either end (Photos 4, 5 and 6).

Photos 4 One end part shaped.

Photos 5 One end completed.

Nature has provided us with an infinite variety of ovoids to emulate, so I try to choose the form that best interacts with the characteristics of each log.

My favourite tool for this is a $\frac{5}{8}$″ gouge, often followed by a $1\frac{1}{4}$″ scraper. I don't worry about tool marks or tear out at this stage.

When I am happy with the final shape I go to work with the sandpaper — lots of it. I start with 60 grit and work down to 80. Perfectionists might even go to 100 grit.

I leave a small knob or stem on each end which is sawn off after the egg comes off the lathe. A little more rounding off with sandpaper on the ends and the egg is complete.

Finishing is done with oil or varnish, as appropriate to your taste and the wood's characteristics, and voila!

Or maybe I should just cluck.

■

Hoop pine.

Osage.

Coco palm.

Manzanita burl.

Finished egg photos by Atomman Kimm.

Photo 6 The finished shape before the stems are sawn off.

Koa.

Turning a Collapsible Beaker

DAVID SPRINGETT

How to turn a watertight, collapsible wooden beaker that fits inside a pocket-size container.

David Springett's interest in woodturning began during the years he was a woodwork teacher. Reading every book then available on the subject (and there were few), trying suggested methods and techniques, experimenting, practising and persevering, he slowly improved his skills.

He became so thoroughly involved in woodturning that 10 years ago he left teaching and since then has earned his living doing what he enjoys most — turning wood.

He specialises in decorated lace bobbins.

would not leave my mind. Working out ideas on paper and eventually on the lathe I recently completed the collapsible beaker you see here. Made from laburnum it shows a rich lustrous finish with its colour ranging from a delicate ginger to black brown. It is a much under-rated British wood.

Wood

Many woods may be chosen for a piece like this but they should be close grained. If the beaker is to be used for drinking it must impart no taste. Boxwood, sycamore or ash might well make suitable substitutes for laburnum, but avoid yew as it is toxic.

The base rim is threaded (using a similar method to that shown in Issue 2 of *Woodturning*) so that the lid screws onto it, but a plain push fit would work equally well. It is the push fitted

When I was a young lad a great uncle gave me what appeared to be a pocket watch, but it wasn't an ordinary pocket watch. When the back opened there were no workings, just a hollow containing a set of concentric tin rings. When you removed these rings and pushed them outwards they telescoped into a small drinking beaker.

Looking through the book *Treen* by Edward Pinto recently I saw illustrated a folding beaker but this time in wood. The photograph was small and indistinct, and the caption was the only indication that the beaker would collapse and telescope just like the metal one I had been given.

From that time onward the idea of making one of these beakers

The pocket 'watch' beaker that so fascinated the young David Springett, with his turned laburnum version

lid which is described below.

The top rim of the beaker is only a few thousandths of an inch smaller in diameter than the threaded rim so that as the collapsed beaker is removed from the cover the top ring lightly clings to the internal sides, telescoping, so that a complete and opened beaker magically appears from the small cover.

To make the beaker and top, cut a 130mm 5⅛″ length by 60mm 2⅜″ square, place it between centres and turn to 55mm 2³/₁₆″. At either end turn a 30mm 1⅛″ length, 35mm 1⅜″ dia. These

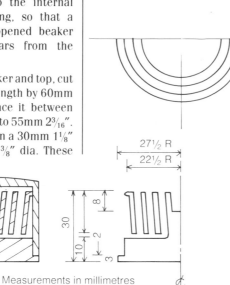
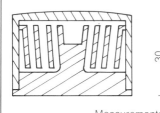

Measurements in millimetres

parts will be held in a 3 jaw chuck so if you decide to hold the work using any other method turn the diameter to suit.

Two pieces

From the headstock end of the wood measure 60mm 2⅜″ and at that point part off. A 5mm ³/₁₆″ width allowance is made for the parting off process. One piece (Part A) is 60mm 2⅜″ long, the other (Part B) is 65mm 2⅝″ long, each with a 30mm 1⅛″ long spigot 35mm 1⅜″ dia.

Remove the driving dog from the headstock and replace it with a 3 jaw chuck. Take Part A, hold the 35mm 1⅜″ dia spigot in the jaws, and bring up the tailstock with a revolving centre in place to support the front face of the work. Ensure that the work runs true and on centre, then square off the face.

From the 55mm 2³/₁₆″ dia shoulder nearest the 3 jaw chuck, measure 3mm ⅛″ towards the tailstock. At that point, and from that point towards the tailstock, turn down to 45mm 1¾″.

On the face, at the tailstock end, mark accurately with a sharp pencil a series of concentric circles whose diameters are: 9mm ¹¹/₃₂″, 13mm ½″, 19mm ¾″, 23mm ⅞″, 29mm 1⅛″, 33mm 1⁵/₁₆″ and 39mm 1⁹/₁₆″.

Parting tool

Now prepare a fine parting tool. An inexpensive 6mm ¼″ woodworking chisel is ideal. Grind, quenching in water regularly, a 30mm 1⅛″ length leaving a 2mm ³/₃₂″ wide blade. If the tool has been overheated it will be necessary to harden and temper it but don't worry for it is a simple process. Using a gas torch, heat the blade to bright red then quickly quench in water. Clean off the black surface bringing the tool to bright metal again. Place the middle of the blade in the flame for a few seconds at a time and it will be noticed that colours begin to appear on the bright metal surface.

These colours, starting with pale straw, brown, then purple and blue can be encouraged to travel along the blade towards the tip by moving the tool in the flame. When the purple colour reaches the tip immediately quench. The more gentle the heating, the wider the band of colour, the more effective the tempering. Now grind the end of the tool sharp as you would a parting tool but do not waste all the time spent tempering by overheating it.

Return to the lathe, withdraw the tailstock and bring the tool rest across the face of the work. Adjust the tool rest so that the

top of the parting tool is at centre height.

Angle

The parting tool has to cut into the face at an angle of 11 deg from the lathe axis. As a guide, fix a strip of masking tape on top of the tool rest and mark upon it in black ink a series of lines with the aid of a protractor or an adjustable bevel set at that angle. The parting tool has to cut to a depth of 20mm ¾″ so, again using a strip of tape, mark a position 20mm ¾″ from the tip of the tool.

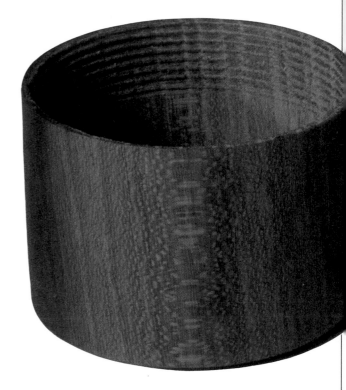

The 11 deg lines are a guide for I feel it is important that the work should not be mechanical and rigid using fixed guides but the tool should be directed by hand and eye.

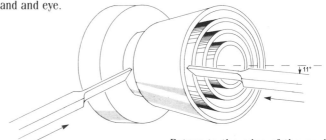

Beginning at the edge move to the area between the 39mm 1⁹/₁₆″ dia and 33mm 1⁵/₁₆″ dia, turn on the lathe, hold the tool

at 11 deg to the face and make the first cut. Withdraw frequently widening the gap from the 2mm ³/₃₂″ cut produced by the tool to the allowed 3mm ⅛″ width. This will ensure that the work does not dangerously grip the tool.

When the depth of cut reaches 20mm ¾″, in line with the tape mark, remove the tool and move to the next cut, between 29mm 1⅛″ dia and 23mm ⅞″. Repeat for the final position between 19mm ¾″ dia and 13mm ½″ dia then move to the centre portion, the 9mm ¹¹/₃₂″ area, which is turned out to a depth of 8mm

⁵/₁₆″, the wall still cut at 11 deg. Clean off the base in the centre and all the deep parting cuts are finished.

Return to the edge of the work and again using the parting tool held at 11 deg trim this outer edge to 20mm ¾″ deep so that the wall thickness is a constant

3mm ⅛". Turn off the lathe and bring the tool rest around parallel to the lathe bed and close to the work.

The beaker shown extended and ready for use

The cylinder sections of the cup have been cut . . .

The outer angled wall must now be turned from 3mm ⅛" thick to 2mm ³⁄₃₂" thick leaving a thicker 3mm ⅛" rounded bead at the top of the rim. When this is finished the beaker walls are complete.

. . . and now parted off

The parted off sections can be seen telescoping out from the base

Parting off

From the 55mm 2³⁄₁₆" dia shoulder nearest the 3 jaw chuck measure 10mm ⅜" (including the 3mm ⅛" shoulder) and draw a line. Switch on the lathe and using the fine parting tool cut in gently until the first rim is parted off. Pull the rim away, fixing it against the angled top of the next part of the beaker wall. Part off the next section and draw that out of the way, then finally part off the third section being careful to stop as soon as it is cut through.

Extend the parts, holding them in place with masking tape if necessary, and shape the inner base of the beaker. No finish is needed for these loosened rims. The piece may now be parted off, with care, behind the 55mm 2³⁄₁₆" dia shoulder nearest the 3 jaw chuck. Lay this part aside and begin work on the lid.

Take Part B and hold the 35mm 1³⁄₈" dia part in the 3 jaw chuck. Bring up the tailstock with revolving centre and ensure the work runs true and on centre. Square off the end face. Remove the revolving centre and replace it with a drill chuck. Fit a 40mm 1⅝" dia saw tooth or forstner bit and drill to a depth of 25mm 1" to remove the bulk of the wood.

Carefully turn the remaining wood so the inside diameter is 45mm 1¾" dia fitting the turned shoulder on piece A accurately. Remember to allow the top rim of the beaker just to clip the inner sides. The depth inside the lid should be 28mm 1⅛".

Fit the turned base into the lid which is still held in the 3 jaw chuck, then replace the drill chuck in the tailstock with a revolving centre bringing it up to support the beaker base. Turn the outer edge of the lid and rim so that they are one. Clean and polish.

Turn the base as close to the centre as possible then remove the centre. Bring the tool rest across the base and complete the turning with light cuts. Clean and polish this surface.

Part off at the top end of the lid placing the almost completed piece to one side while a jam chuck is made. Turn the jam chuck with a 45mm 1¾" shoulder. Fit the lid on it, lightly supporting the end with a revolving centre. Turn as much of the lid top as possible with the centre in place providing support. Finally move it away, bring the tool rest across the face and with light cuts complete the lid top. Clean and polish the lid, then re-fit it on to the base.

The beaker in its collapsed form

I have tested the beaker and it is water-tight. In fact when liquid is poured into it it swells and the joints become so tight it is difficult to collapse. Allow it to dry out a little before folding it down.

Constant use may cause the wood to move and the joints might leak, so the choice of a stable wood is essential. It is one of those pieces which can be carried in the pocket and brought out to surprise and delight friends. ∎

The beaker is collapsed inside its container with a 50p coin for size comparison

Rien Blomsma began his working life with Shell at The Hague but his new career was broken off by the German invasion of Holland. Expecting the war to end soon he took a temporary job with the Dutch coal distribution bureau, but this lasted five years.

Living near the German anti-tank canal and zone cut through The Hague, and not far from a launching site of V-2 rockets, the 'hunger winter' 1944/45 was unpleasant.

In 1946 he found his vocation in a technical import business. Selling Union Carbide plastics raw materials, he grew up with the Dutch plastics, coatings and glue industries. This made him critical of bad plastic mouldings.

After moving to Rotterdam and setting up his own firm he also sold cargo heating coils for crude oil tankers, fuel-oil additives for steamships, synthetic roofing sheeting for large buildings and special lubricants for all kinds of machinery.

At home he gradually built up a workshop to counter-balance "making a living with my tongue and my fountain-pen".

Besides hand tools he has an American circular saw, Austrian bandsaw, German drills and router, Myford metal lathe, self-built wood lathe, and a bench drill produced in Hiroshima — a real United Nations in tools.

Rien retired seven years ago and is regularly asked by family and friends to make or repair a variety of things.

ANGULAR TURNINGS

RIEN BLOMSMA

You do not need a huge workshop with fancy equipment to experiment with new ideas and techniques, as a Dutch reader shows with this simple project he made in his flat.

I turn wood seldom and I am just a beginner. The only advantage my article might have is to serve as a counterweight for the marvellous turnings shown by international celebrities, whose work might intimidate some newcomers.

So I ask the professionals to please start reading elsewhere in this issue, and I will talk for a few moments to beginners like myself.

I do not live in a residential area with a two-car garage converted into a woodworking workshop. My crowded workshop is a small spare room in a third-floor city apartment.

Moreover I am totally left-handed so what I do you can do much better if you stick to it.

A few years ago I had just acquired a hand power drill turning set, and was making my first attempts at turning between centres, when my brother-in-law asked me for two dozen small (70mm 2¾") spindles with a fancy profile. These were for an old cabinet which a friend of his had bought cheaply with a broken railing.

When I finally handed them over there were sufficient variations to justify the guarantee 'hand-made'. It felt like an achievement and, carried away, I decided to get a wood turning lathe.

At the time the only ones obtainable in Holland were industrial machines with corresponding prices, weights and space requirements. As I had an old Myford screwcutting lathe I started to build a wood lathe, based on plans from an old Dutch DIY book. I had to spread this out over many months.

My daily job was rather demanding, and after the lathe was finally completed there were long intervals between turning sessions. Apart from a table lamp stand and a number of things for my wife and friends, I could not bring myself to making the peppermills or finials sketched in a book I had acquired by then.

Craving one day to find something interesting to make I got an idea — how about a combination of straight sides and turned round parts? After much thinking and scribbling on paper I decided on a 6-sided pyramid, and after putting that on the lathe I would see what else I could do with it.

To produce a pyramid you need a bandsaw (or a friend with one).

I used a simple piece of elm which I happened to have. After turning a decent cylinder slightly larger than needed, I drew a circle at one end with compasses and pencil. By marking off the radius six times around the circumference and connecting the six points by straight lines I obtained a hexagon.

The cylinder was then mounted horizontally between two short vertical pillars, both erected on a small piece of wood — 19mm ¾" plywood is fine.

The cylinder was attached to the pillars with screws through the centres at both ends, and one side of the drawn hexagon had to be exactly vertical, because that is where the bandsaw started cutting (FIG 1).

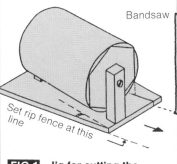
Bandsaw

Set rip fence at this line

FIG 1 Jig for cutting the straight sides.

If the sides of the plywood sheet were parallel with the axis of the wooden cylinder, bandsawing would result in a

"Take care not to make my mistake of forgetting the inside depth when turning the foot. I cut through to the inside and ruined the whole thing."

Rien's spare room workshop in his flat.

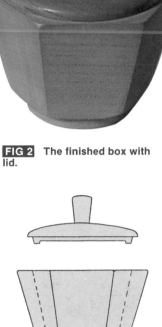

FIG 2 The finished box with lid.

6-sided prism. To make a pyramid the guiding side of the plywood sheet must make an angle with the cylinder axis. How large an angle will depend on your design. In my case it was about 12 DEG.

After making one cut, turn the cylinder until the next hexagon line is vertical, fasten both screws and cut the second side, and so on until your truncated pyramid is ready. If you have worked carefully for each step, the result will show identical trapeziums on all sides.

Pyramid

Having mounted the narrower end of my pyramid with screws on a wooden disc attached to a faceplate, I decided to hollow it as a box and give it a round foot.

Take care not to make my mistake of forgetting the inside depth when turning the foot. I cut through to the inside and ruined the whole thing. However, I succeeded in repairing it.

The bottomless box was mounted on a wooden disc with a raised central part to fit just inside the wide circular mouth, and six pieces of bevelled wood were nailed on the disc to clamp the six sides. In this way the smaller part of the pyramid could be turned to accept a new foot, which was turned separately with a rabbet and glued on.

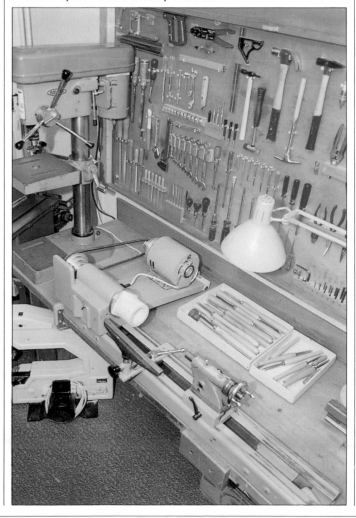

To complete the box I turned a lid and attached a small knob with a dowel (FIG 2).

Needless to say, this method will serve to produce turnings with a different number of straight sides, low boxes or bowls, or tall and slim vases.

The straight part may also be a smaller portion of the total height. Also the sharpness of the angles may be partly removed by turning, or by sanding while the lathe is turning. The narrower part of the pyramid may be at the top instead of at the bottom, or you may make a prism instead of a pyramid.

In short, there are endless opportunities for you to experiment. ■

Ray Hopper left school at 14 to take up an apprenticeship as a printing press engineer. But he decided he would rather earn a living as a woodworker.

He worked at a joiners' shop while studying at the East Ham College of Building for his City and Guilds qualifications in carpentry and joinery, and has since worked in many disciplines of wood including more than 30 years as a foreman in a woodworking shop.

A self-taught woodturner (he bought an old metal-spinning lathe and taught himself to turn tool handles and bowls from elm offcuts), he is keen to teach and to pass on his knowledge, and has held seminars and classes on multi-centre woodturning in Britain and abroad.

He is a member of the Ely Guild of Woodturners, and is married with two grown-up daughters.

The hat in the photograph was turned from one piece of horse chestnut, and the stick from a cherrywood branch.

Turn a triangular bud vase

Two finished vases.

FIG 2 Forming a taper.

RAY HOPPER

This unusual project for the experienced woodturner is taken from Ray's new book *Multi-centre Woodturning* which was published by GMC Publications in October 1992, and reviewed in *Woodturning* Issue 11 (Nov/Dec).

The wood for the bud vase needs to be 75mm 3" square and about 180mm 7" long. A 100mm 4" x 15mm ⅝" glass phial to hold water for the flower bud should be available at most craft supply outlets, although you can make your own from a suitable piece of plastic or metal tube. The bottom of the tube can be sealed with silicone mastic, which can be purchased in small tubes from an ironmonger.

The following method could also be used on a dried grass vase, but the wood would then have to be proportionally larger.

First mark both ends of the wood with a true centre mark —

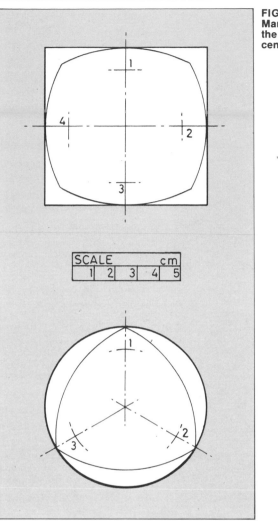

FIG 1 Marking out the true centres.

SCALE | cm
1 2 3 4 5

FIG 1 illustrates setting out on the base of both a triangular vase and a square vase.

For this project, mark the base with the three points shown in the illustration, and make a saw cut across these points to receive the wings of the drive spur.

Now place the wood between centres on the lathe, using the true centres, and turn the whole length to a cylindrical shape with a roughing gouge, at a speed of about 1800 RPM.

Cut away some of the wood to form a taper towards the tailstock from about halfway along the cylinder, as shown in FIG 2. This will help you to visualise the final shape of the vase when you multi-turn the lower part.

Change the lathe speed to a slower speed, about 700 RPM, and mount the wood on to one of the off-centre marks, having numbered the off-centre locations 1, 2 and 3. As you will be remounting the work a few times, this will help you select the correct centre for each cut.

Revolve the lathe by hand to ensure the work clears the

FIG 3 The spigot turned.

FIG 4 Boring a hole for the water holder.

toolrest before making a cut parallel with the toolrest, which should itself be parallel with the lathe bed.

Repeat the cut on off-centres 2 and 3 and, if necessary, remount the work on any of the off-centre marks until there is a triangular shape as in FIG 1.

Using the toolrest as a guide,

make three lines along the length of the wood at the corners of the triangle (FIG 2).

At this stage you will need to go back to centres 1, 2 and 3 to make the final finishing cuts. First go back to off-centre 1 and remove some wood with a skew chisel until you have cut up to the lines. You may have to stop the lathe a few times to do this accurately.

Rest the index finger of the hand supporting the tool blade against the toolrest and try to make flowing cuts — it may be helpful to use a scraper on the final cuts.

The three faces can now be sandpapered while the lathe is stationary. Wrap fine sandpaper round a block and hold it flat on the surface to prevent the corners of the triangular section becoming rounded over.

Drilling

The vase needs to be mounted in a spigot chuck or a three-jaw chuck for drilling to receive the water holder. Place the vase in the lathe using the true centres, and turn the spigot (FIG 3).

Remember that once you have turned the spigot you will have lost the multi-centre locations, and you will not be able to do any more work on the triangular section.

Now mount the work in the spigot chuck or three-jaw chuck, and at a low speed bore a hole to receive the water holder, using a sawtooth bit mounted in a chuck in the tailstock (FIG 4).

This photograph also illustrates a multi-centre handle I made from mahogany for the tailstock. This gives me greater control and leverage when boring holes on the lathe in this manner.

Place a revolving centre in the tailstock and wind it into the water container hole, to provide support while you shape and finish the project.

Once you have mastered the techniques and principle, you can experiment and perhaps add some decorative turning. ∎

Having inlaid wood with all kinds of materials, ranging from leather and veneer to contrasting bands of sawdust, I thought, "Why not use ground minerals as a form of decoration, especially those that retain a vivid colour when pulverised?"

Turquoise was the first that came to mind, possibly because I grew up in the turquoise mining and jewellery area of the south western United States.

While visiting Albuquerque, New Mexico, to watch Alan Lacer demonstrate, I found a supplier of both turquoise gravel and powder, and was able to buy a small batch for starters. Unfortunately, he became unreliable after the first shipment.

In 1992, I started searching for suppliers in Arizona, Colorado, New Mexico and Nevada, where the main US turquoise mines are found. The search was fruitful.

Several Arizona mines produce a beautiful, light blue, clear turquoise, and those in Nevada and New Mexico a stunning dark blue or green gemstone, many with other materials embedded, including pyrites, which flashes in the finished matrix.

About the same time, after inspecting native American Indian jewellery, it became clear that mixing red coral with turquoise would splendidly highlight the blue.

Since turquoise relates to the south western United States, it seemed appropriate to pattern bowls after the pottery of indian tribes, such as the Hopi, Zuni, Acoma/Laguna, San Ildefonso, Santa Clara, Taos, and Maricopa.

This has worked well, especially on pieces made from soft woods my wife and I gather near our Rocky Mountain home, including aspen, pine, piñon pine, and aromatic red cedar.

But the turquoise and coral colours beautifully enhance any

Born and raised in the Colorado Rockies, Dave Kahne entered the Army Air Corps in 1943 and was a pilot with Bomber Command, near Peterborough, in World War Two.
After demob in 1945, he entered the building materials business. But he was recalled to active duty in 1951, completed his engineering degree, and later flew 176 missions in Vietnam, retiring from the USAF in 1971.
He was vice president of a commercial bank and now owns a successful commercial real estate business.
Dave has been turning wood as a hobby for about five years and plans to become a full time turner by the end of next year. He has been happily married for 49 years, has three children and eight grandchildren.
*Dave Kahne,
1709 Person Street,
Laramie,
Wyoming 82070,
USA.*

turning

DAVE KAHNE

Woodturners are always looking for ways to decorate their 'works of art.' Dave Kahne decided to use pulverised ground minerals, chiefly turquoise and coral, to adorn his.

yellow or red woods, especially osage orange, pau amarello, pau cetim, padauk, bubinga and all the mahoganies.

The first stage to inlay a turning, once your vessel has been roughed to final shape, is to cut channels to receive the turquoise and coral. Photo 1 shows these channels cut in the lip and body of the bowl.

I use Henry Taylor's modified parting tool 3mm ⅛" x 19mm ¾" x 150mm 6" long, which allows you to vary the width and depth easily. Then remove the workpiece from the lathe.

My wife and I conducted numerous experiments with different adhesives. G-2 Epoxy proved too difficult to control. You cannot insert small

amounts, like drops, and it runs all over the workpiece. It also dries too slowly and darkens the turquoise powder to a muddy colour.

Woodworker glues (yellow and white) won't work due to colour and lack of heat resistance. Cyanoacrylate (CA) glues can withstand temperatures up to 177 DEG C (350 DEG F) dry quite clear and can be machined.

As viscosity is important to securely set matrix particles, we find it helps to mix the CA glues. Water-thin CA (red label), with a viscosity of five, is too thin, but the gap-filling (yellow label) with a viscosity of 300 is too thick.

Try mixing one part of red label to five parts yellow. When your yellow label bottle is half empty (or half full, if you're an optimist), pour in about one-

Photo 1
Channels are cut into the workpiece to receive inlay materials.

Aspen, turquoise and coral bowl
with Indian pictograph symbols, 53mm 2⅛" x 113mm 4½" DIA.

TURQUOISE

Aspen vessel
with turquoise and coral, Indian pictograph symbols in turquoise and coral, 133mm 5¼" x 150mm 6" DIA.

Spalted birch and oak box
with turquoise and coral, 190mm 7½" x 117mm 4⅝" DIA.

fifth of that amount from the red bottle.

The proportions are not critical, but it needs to be thin enough to run under the particles and chunks, yet not so thin that it dries immediately or soaks into the wood. Label the bottle 'Mix.'

Stage two is to lay in the inlay matrix, after first spreading a large sheet of newspaper on the workbench. If using coral, put four to six pieces where desired in the channel and put one or two drops of mixed CA glue on them.

Put away the coral and pour some turquoise fragments onto the paper. Either place this into the channel with a small spoon or individually place pieces with tweezers.

We use both light and dark turquoise, mixing them in between the coral pieces. After the channel is filled, spread the glue mixture liberally over the material, so it spreads around the pieces — but not so much that it runs over the side of your bowl.

Set the workpiece aside for a moment, fold the paper and pour the unused turquoise back into the container. Using this method, not one particle of the expensive turquoise or coral is ever wasted.

Spread the paper again, and using the spoon, pour turquoise powder liberally on every part of the channel. Tap the workpiece gently on the bench (over the paper) or with the handle of the spoon (over the paper) to shake the powder down into the glue-filled voids between the chunks of turquoise, and the excess, dry, powder onto the paper.

You might have to do this twice to fill some spaces. The powder will soak up much of the CA glue, but not quite enough. Set the workpiece aside for a moment, carefully fold the paper, and pour the excess turquoise back into the container so you don't waste any.

Retrieve the workpiece and carefully soak the fragments on top of the channel with water-thin CA glue (red label), one ▶

'Several Arizona mines produce a beautiful light blue, clear turquoise, and those in Nevada and New Mexico a stunning dark blue or green gemstone.'

Photo 2 The rough turquoise and coral matrix is applied to the workpiece.

(same as a good quality file, which is how you test the hardness of a stone), it will be difficult to sand and polish. Our nephew uses jasper and rhyolite, and it works well. Don't use agate, quartz, emeralds or diamonds.

The third stage is to sand down the matrix. Turquoise has a Mohs hardness of about five. Garnet paper doesn't last long with such punishment, so silicon carbide or aluminium oxide are preferable.

Experiments with various adhesives, grinding and sanding materials, lathe speeds and bowl shapes were carried out. Soft woods erode rapidly when power sanding, and quickly become depressions around the harder turquoise.

The solution is to initially sand the inlay with either the sandpaper or the workpiece at rest. Photo 3 shows the start of sanding the lip, with the sanding disc at its lowest speed, using a grit of 80 or higher. Very coarse

Photo 3 Sanding the turquoise and coral matrix flush with the surface of the workpiece.

drop at a time, but not so much as to run over your bowl and stain the wood or stick your fingers to it.

If desired, you can then spray with accelerator to harden, but it's best to allow the glue to harden overnight. Photo 2 shows the workpiece after the glue has dried. As you can see, it's an ugly, sharp-edged, hard mess.

We use the light blue Arizona turquoise, pulverise it in a home-made hammer mill designed and built by our nephew turner, then sift it into coarse and fine grades. The coarse is excellent for the lip or any narrow channels.

Other minerals can be used, but hardness is a major consideration. If much harder than 6.5 on the Mohs scale

Cherry footed bowl with turquoise, coral, 92mm 3⅝" x 245mm 9⅝" DIA.

Desert Sunrise, aromatic red cedar, turquoise, coral, turquoise cabochon, 85mm 3¼" x 95mm 3¾" DIA.

grits tear the turquoise out of the channel.

Remount the workpiece, but do not turn on the lathe. Install 100 or 120 grit sandpaper on Powerlok or Velcro holders, 75mm 3″ or 125mm 5″ DIA and slowly, carefully, sand the excess turquoise until the division between wood and turquoise is sharply defined.

Sandpaper disc life can be extended by powering the disc against a sandpaper cleaner stick. Check occasionally for material being torn from the matrix by the sandpaper.

If the holes are large, fill them with powder, wet down with CA water-thin (red label) glue, and use accelerator on the spot. If small, fill them with CA yellow or green label glue, spray on some accelerator, and put the piece back on the lathe to finish sanding.

If you want to install silver wire, a leather thong, or inlay banding on the bowl as well, this should be done before

> ## 'Coral is becoming very difficult to obtain, as in some areas it is an endangered species . . . and can no longer be harvested.'

using the 120 grit.

When all the excess turquoise has been ground away, turn on the lathe at low speed, move up to the next higher grade of paper and sand the turquoise and wood together.

After 150 or 180 grit, increase the lathe speed to around 700 to 900 RPM. We suggest you use every grit up to 320.

Increase RPM to about 1100, then continue with 400, 600, 800 and even 1200 grit on only the turquoise. This will give the inlay a final, lustrous polish. Photo 4 shows the entire sanding completed, before final finishing. ▶

Photo 4 The sanding and initial polishing of the matrix and embedding of silver wire is completed. Final finishing and polishing of the wood and matrix remains.

Nutmeg vessel
with turquoise and coral inlay. Bad checks have been filled with turquoise, 90mm 3½″ x 180mm 7″ DIA.

The completed aspen,
turquoise, coral and silver bowl used as an example in the article, 88mm 3⅜″ x 155mm 6⅛″ DIA.

Aspen vessel
with red cedar base and top liner, turquoise and coral, 135mm 5¼″ x 240mm 9½″ DIA.

For this we use one coat of 50/50 diluted lacquer as a sealer-filler, applied lavishly, then wiped dry after a few seconds. A second light coat of lacquer is sprayed on, allowing 10 or more minutes to dry thoroughly.

Then the lathe is turned on, the speed increased, and it is buffed with a hand-held soft cloth until shiny and smooth. Stop the lathe and let the lacquer cool from buffing.

For our final finish we apply HUT, a silicon wax product, at a relatively high speed (1600-1800 RPM). It is then buffed with a cloth held firmly against the surface.

This generates considerable heat (so watch your fingers), which drives the HUT into the wood. A final soft buffing with a clean, soft cloth provides an incomparable finish.

HUT is made by Tom Hutchinson in Missouri, and sold mainly through American woodturning suppliers.

Turquoise suppliers sell in either large or small quantities, depending on whether they are miners, wholesalers or retailers.

It costs about US$6 (£4) for one ounce, depending on the quality, size, colour, and preparation. But an ounce of turquoise goes a long way.

Coral is a different story. It is becoming very difficult to obtain, as in some areas it is an endangered species — yes, it is a living organism — and can no longer be harvested.

Large pieces are seldom sold, since they can be machined into jewellery, but the nice thing about using it to decorate woodturnings is we only need bits and pieces not suitable for jewellery.

Any readers interested in this kind of inlaying, who include money for postage and a self-addressed envelope, can obtain from me a list of turquoise and silver suppliers, who may also have coral.

I hope this feature and the accompanying photos will give you an insight into the possibilities of inlaying with minerals.

Ed's note: Craft Supplies and John Boddy both stock Hot Stuff adhesive, the instant CA glue. ∎

Aspen vessel

with turquoise and coral inlay. Defects filled with turquoise, 95mm 3¾" x 160mm 6¼" DIA.

Bracelet
made from osage orange, with turquoise, coral, veneer inlay banding, 15mm ⅝" x 65mm 2⅝" DIA.

Honduras rosewood lidded vessel,
turquoise, coral, 160mm 6¼" x 100mm 4" DIA.

MUSHROOM

Magic

Spot the real mushrooms and toadstools.

PAUL PEETERS

Fungi are like snakes. Some are harmless, others highly poisonous. They come in all colours, shapes and sizes, are difficult to distinguish and have a repellent fascination. Paul Peeters describes how to turn these strange, mysterious plants.

Autumn is here. And the woods and fields are full of fungi, those colourful, leafless, fleshy plants so beloved of witch and dwarf-inhabited fairytales. Finding some while out for a walk in the woods gave me the idea to turn wooden mushrooms and toadstools.

I began to seek, and draw, various shapes and sizes, some with smooth skins and pale 'hats', others with rough skins and poisonous-looking spotted vermilion caps. Round and pointed tops, long and short, thick and thin and so on.

Back home, I decided they would be ideal subjects for using up those small branches I can never bear to burn. My shed is full of these, mainly timber from fruit trees, yew and golden rain (laburnum). I always think that one day they'll be useful.

First I cut them into logs ▶

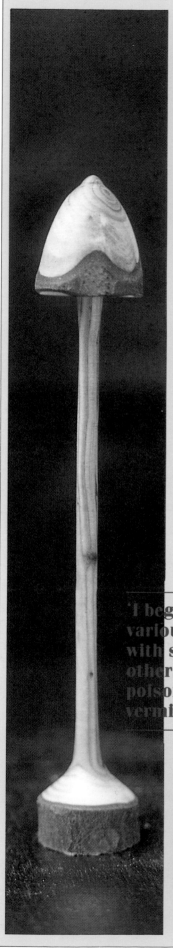

Branches were cut into small logs.

The start — and the finish.

Secure the log in a four-jaw chuck.

'I began to seek out, and draw, various shapes and sizes, some with smooth skins and pale hats, others with rough skins and poisonous-looking spotted vermilion caps.'

Start by turning the hat.

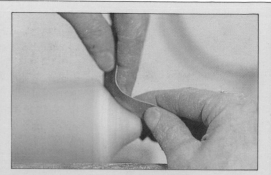

Sand the hat before making the foot.

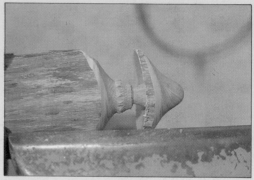

Undercut the hat or it looks too heavy.

Turning the foot.

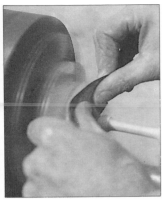
Parting off the mushroom.

Sanding the foot and the base.

Undercut the base a little.

Cleaning up the base.

The finished mushroom.

some 100-200mm 4"-8" long and class them according to diameter. Then I secure a piece, more or less circular, on a four-jaw chuck, with a lathe speed of 2,800 RPM.

Next, I begin to turn the hat of the mushroom, sanding this before making the foot, as a thin base can break if you sand it later.

I determine the shape of the base by boring under (under-cutting) the hat. If the wood isn't circular, the shape gets wavy and looks more natural. If I don't bore beneath the hat it looks too heavy.

While making the foot, I can create a rough neck by pushing the gouge towards the hat. The base of the foot can be made rough or smooth.

To make it rough, I repeatedly push the gouge on the side towards the base. The foot can look separated or integrated to the base.

Then I sand the smooth parts of the foot and the base. To part off the mushroom from the lathe, I hold it lightly by the foot on a smooth section, using my right hand thumb and forefinger. I take special care around the neck of the hat and the rough sections.

I part the base with a thin tool (grain d'orge in French), pushing to the right, to bore the base slightly. To finish, I use a bit of teak oil — or nothing.

If you plan to make a mushroom and want a variation, try turning one which bends. First you turn the hat. Then you grip the chuck and hit the piece of wood to uncentre it.

You grip the chuck again and turn the foot. So the hat and foot won't be in the same axis.

Another variation is to turn the whole mushroom and to change the centre before parting it from the lathe. So the base hasn't the same centre as the mushroom and looks as though it's leaning.

To conclude: mushrooms are cheap to make, quick and easy — you can easily produce about 10 an hour — because you can create any shape you like, according to the wood.

As my teacher said, when I was a child drawing all kinds of shapes and colours of fish: "There are so many kinds of fish in the oceans that yours almost certainly exists." It's the same with mushrooms.

Paul Peeters at the lathe.

Since I started adding my mushrooms (and business cards) to the chestnuts and leaves used to decorate autumnal shop windows, I have become quite famous in my town. People will come up to me in the streets and say: "You're the mushroom man, aren't you?" I'm proud to say I am. ■

There are plenty of turning subjects in the kitchen.

Mushrooms come in all shapes and sizes.

Ernie Conover is our contributing editor in America. He teaches woodworking in general, and woodturning in particular, at Conover Workshops, a school he and his wife Susan operate together. In addition to writing and lecturing widely, he is a technical consultant to a number of companies on design and manufacture of woodworking tools and machines.

Pepper Mills

ERNIE CONOVER

Not a project to sneeze at!

Any cook appreciates the gastronomical value that freshly ground pepper adds to a meal. The pre-ground variety is just weak tea by comparison. It is like the difference between a freshly caught trout and frozen fish sticks. The trouble is that a decent pepper grinder goes down for a minimum of 40 bucks at the local kitchen implement store. They take two forms, tacky plastic monstrosities and more expensive machine turned wood examples. It is difficult to find sufficient pejoratives to describe the wood and the turning in the average store-bought pepper mill. Let's leave it at abysmal in both cases.

With the above in mind, it is clear that turning a pepper mill, and possibly a matching salt shaker, makes a great turning project. Seeing as the necessary hardware costs between $6 and $12, the project is also economically viable. With some easily made chucks and gauges it is a snap to turn out pepper mills and salt shakers in quantity. A local kitchen implement store would probably be glad to buy them for $20 to $30 each, especially if you use some interesting wood.

Mechanisms

In researching sources for this article, I found that there were a surprising number of mechanisms available. None of them, however, matched the

quality available in the past. Rude Osolnik has a set he made in the 1950s with mechanisms by Thompson Brothers in California that exhibit aerospace quality. Sadly such quality does not seem to be available today, but more about this as we progress.

All of the mechanisms work along much the same line as outlined in our drawing. By turning the cap, the central shift is turned, which turns the grinder itself in the serrated outer bezel. The grinder has

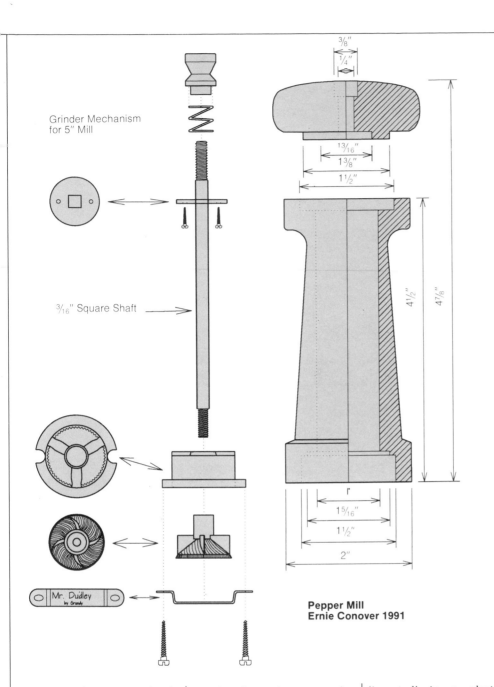

Grinder Mechanism
for 5″ Mill

3/16″ Square Shaft

Mr. Dudley
by Grundy

Pepper Mill
Ernie Conover 1991

and weaknesses which I will elaborate on as we progress. The first was a mechanism made by Grundy in California, USA and sold as the Mr Dudley. It is available from Craft Supplies, USA, 1287 E. 1120 S., Provo, UT 84601, USA, Phone (801) 373-0917 and Woodworkers Store, 21801 Industrial Blvd, Rogers, MN 55374-9514, USA, Phone (612) 428-2199 for $6.50. It had an investment cast grinder and bezel, but exhibited good workmanship throughout and even one innovation. Since it was the first mechanism I obtained it is the one I drew for this discourse. It is typical of all the mechanisms.

The Mr Dudley uses a spring to control the end play in the grinder. That is the amount of distance between the serrations of the grinder and bezel, which controls the size of grind. All other mechanisms I have seen control this by how tight the top crown nut is tightened. As the top is turned, however, this nut works loose and constant adjustment is impossible. **Being machinists, my father and I have always turned a threaded brass washer to go under the crown nut. This provides a double nut that locks the amount of end play precisely.**

The Mr Dudley mechanism overcomes this problem with a spring which holds constant tension on the grinder. It is a nice solution. Additionally the Mr Dudley is all steel and nicely plated. I find the plated steel crown nut a bit offensive as my instinct is to knurled brass. I generally turn my own from this material.

The next mechanism I obtained for the article was from Craft Supplies Ltd, The Millers Dale, Nr Buxton, Derbyshire SK17 8SN, UK, Phone (0298) 871636. I asked for their best quality mill which is written up in the catalogue as 'machined steel mechanism' at a cost of £2.70. The mill that arrived here in Ohio was indeed machined steel and nicely plated. What is more, the crown nut was brass. Since it did not

serrations that mate closely with those of the bezel, but also has spiral channels (or paddles in the Mr Dudley) to direct the peppercorns down into the area where the actual grinding takes place. These channels are tapered to provide the crushing action necessary to grind the peppercorns.

In a good mechanism the serrations in both the grinder and the bezel are machined. Since the serrations and the channels are asymmetrical, machining them cleanly, and with sharp edges, is no mean task. Enter stage right modern technology in the form of investment casting. To invest-

ment cast a part, an expensive die is made which can mould the part out of wax. Such a die would cost upward of $5000 and would mould a wax part that was slightly larger than the part we want to cast from metal. The amount oversize is done to a shrink formula which precisely predicts the amount the metal will shrink when it cools from the molten to solid state.

The mould is attached to an injection moulding machine, really designed for the plastic industry. It spits out our wax master parts like popcorn. The parts are then attached to a central wax shaft forming what is called a tree. The tree is then

'invested' in a plaster-like material which is allowed to harden. The plaster mould is then heated in an autoclave and the wax melts out of the cavities. Molten steel is now poured into the mould. Once cool the mould is broken leaving perfect parts which are dimensionally perfect.

While investment casting makes possible mass production of grinding mechanisms, it does not produce the crisp, sharp edges to the serrations that machining does. The result is pepper that is more crushed than ground.

I tested three mechanisms for this article. All had strengths have any maker's name or country of manufacture, I could not guess where it was made. The mechanism had the most parts of any tested and required more stepped recesses between the cap and the body which requires more turning.

The third and final grinder I tested was the Zassenhaus made in West Germany — now Germany. I obtained it from Woodcraft Supply Corp, PO Box 1686, Parkersburg, WV 26102-1686, USA, Phone (304) 428-8261. Woodcraft's price for the 150mm 6″ model is $9.95. It was exquisitely machined, absolutely perfect — what we would expect from the Germans. It also had a nicely machined and knurled brass crown nut. The Zassenhaus was also the easiest from a turning standpoint, requiring only a 27mm (1.063″) hole through the body with a 37mm (1.457″) recess for the grinder. The cap only requires an 11mm (.433″) hole. The ease of turning is because the Zassenhaus uses a lot of plastic. A plastic wrapping around the bezel fits into the 27mm hole and 37mm recess. Another plastic bearing supports the shaft just under the lid. Finally a nylon insert in the 11mm hole turns the cap into a nut which turns the shaft. Although this is high quality plastic (nylon and duerlon), it just bothers me a bit in a hand turned wood pepper mill. Still, it works well, is machined to perfection and is super easy from a woodturning standpoint.

As a postscript on mechanisms, I might add that in our kitchen is a mass produced mill that was given to us. It has a French mechanism marked Peugeot Freres, Lion. It is of very high quality with machined grinder and bezel and all metal. The crown nut is plated steel. If anyone can find a source for the handiwork of the Peugeot brothers, I would like to know. A word of warning, when trying to read the print on a mechanism: **don't blow the pepper dust away as I just did. It ends up in your eyes and**

mouth. Pepper alone seems to lack certain epicurean value and burns the eyes, verily as I type.

As a post, postscript all of the mechanims mentioned above, except the Mr Dudley, suffer from end play problems. The only solution is to turn your own locknut.

Turning the Body

Turning the body is straight spindle turning. Start by selecting a suitable square of timber and cutting the ends dead square in the table saw and to the desired length. This is a job where accurately dimensioned and squared timber makes life simpler. I like to select burl or wild grained woods for mills. For this article I made 125mm (5″) mills so the body was 114.3mm (4½″) long. I also try to find timber that will yield me a bit better than the 50.8mm (2″) major diameter required for the project. Something on the order of 54mm (2⅛″) or 57mm (2¼″) gives some room for centring errors and such.

Now find centre by drawing diagonals on the ends and centrepunch the intersections. If you have a drill press, it provides the easiest way to drill the central core hole through the body. This is why accurately squared ends are important. If you do not possess a drill press, take heart, for your lathe is a perfectly good drill press. It's just that it's lying on its side. You need a drill pad which can easily be turned from wood to fit the Morse taper into your tailstock. I have provided a rough sketch to work from. It turns your tailstock spindle into a mini drill press table. In our lathe drill press the table now goes up and down instead of the quill.

The easiest way to get the wooden Morse taper on our drill pad just right is to use our tailstock as a gauge. Turn the taper close to size then wipe a chalk mark longitudinally down the length of the taper. Now

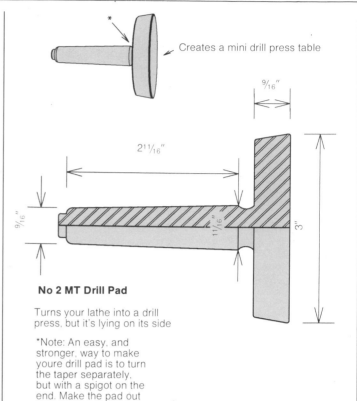

Creates a mini drill press table

No 2 MT Drill Pad

Turns your lathe into a drill press, but it's lying on its side

*Note: An easy, and stronger, way to make youre drill pad is to turn the taper separately, but with a spigot on the end. Make the pad out of ½″ or ¾″ plywood, drill to spigot size and glue together.

insert the wooden taper in the spindle until it seats. See if it rocks and twist it about one quarter turn. By how the chalk smears you will be able to see what to remove and what to keep. Make the drill pad out of a fairly sturdy wood such as maple and spindle turn it. By turning between centres you will be able to chuck and unchuck repeatedly without loosing concentricity. To face the flat for the pad you can chuck the Morse taper in the headstock and use a scraper, insuring that the table is square with the axis of the Morse taper.

Chuck a drill of the core diameter in the headstock, hold the work firmly on your newly made drill pad with your left hand, turn the lathe on at a moderate speed (200 to 600 rpm) and slowly advance the tailstock ram with your right hand. **Do be careful that the drill does not wander out of the work and into your hand.** Whether done on the lathe or in a real drill press, I like to drill equal distance from each end, meeting in the middle as best

as possible. Since we are drilling into end grain, most drills have a tendency to wander — following the grain. By drilling from both ends we minimise this by averaging the err . For our Mr Dudley Mill in the drawing the core hole is 25.4mm (1″). For the Craft Supplies Ltd. Mill the core diameter would be 24mm (.945″) while the Zassenhaus would be 27mm (1.063″).

The various recesses in both the top and the bottom of the body can be drilled with Forstner bits. This is a good way if you are going to crank out a production run. If you use this method you will have to start with the biggest bit first at each end and work down to the core diameter to maintain centring.

I prefer to mount the freshly drilled body on an expansion mandrel and scrape the recesses with a small right-angle scraper. Such a scraper can be made from an old file and is depicted in my article *Making a Box* on page 36 of Issue Number 4 of **Woodturning**. This leaves precise square shoulders that are cosmetically superior to drill work. It is also just as fast if you turn some wood 'go' gauges of the recess diameters. Such a gauge is often called a plug gauge. Simply scrape until the gauge just goes into the recess. A gauge will also help greatly in turning recesses that are straight rather than tapered.

The expansion mandrel is also easy to make, as it is straight spindle turning. Mount a suit-

saw kerf in a small drilled hole to help prevent splitting. I have never found it makes much difference.

To use our new chuck, slide the freshly drilled body onto the mandrel and tap the tapered plug home. You may have to use a small length of dowel as a ram rod to do this. You can now scrape the recesses and turn the outside to a design that suits your taste. To do the other

centre diameters with a cutoff tool. Whether this is faceplate turning or spindle turning is merely a question of how you orient the grain. I now jam chuck the piece and face the end. I now drill the cap to the core diameter which would be 6.35mm (¼″) in the Mr Dudley Mechanism in our drawing. It would be 5mm (.197″) for the Craft Supplies Ltd. mechanism and 11mm (.433″) for the

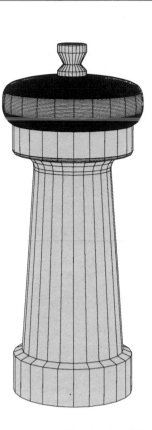

The Finished Mill

Hardwood screwed end grain to a faceplate with 1″ long No 12 sheet metal screws

⅝″

3¼″

2″

1″

⅜″

Expansion Mandrel

Back saw two places to create four slots, which allows mandrel to expand

1⁹⁄₁₆″

⁷⁄₁₆″

Small plug turned to approximately 3° taper fits into similarly turned recess in mandrel and expands mandrel to grip work

Make tapered hole in mandrel by first through drilling ⅜″ and then scraping taper. A dowel can be inserted from back through faceplate to remove plug and work

able block of timber on a faceplate, remembering to screw into the end grain because we are spindle turning. I like to use 25.4mm (1″) No 12 sheet metal screws, which hold far better than common wood screws. Turn the mandrel and a square shoulder up to it. Next bore through the centre of the mandrel and out the back with a 10mm (⅜″) drill. Scrape a 3° (1½° per side) taper into the mandrel and turn a mating tapered plug to fit as per our drawing. Our chalk trick will aid in this fit. All that is left to do is to back saw the mandrel in quarters so that it can expand. Some workers like to end the

end simply reverse the work on the mandrel. This method insures perfect concentricity between the core hole and all other elements of the turning process.

Turning the Cap

While most workers generally faceplate turn the cap, it can just as well be spindle turned — the choice is yours. I use a jam chuck but a metal chuck will also work. For more on jam chucks see my article *Lathe Chucking* on page 33 of Issue Number 1 of **Woodturning**. I turn to rough diameter between centres and face the ends

square to the spur centre/dead Zassenhaus.

After drilling, scrape the shoulders and test the fit with the body. Knock the piece out of the jam chuck and reverse, now chucking on the recess. If you are doing a production run it is nice to have several jam chucks each turned to the diameter in question. I now turn the outside profile of the cap and scrape any counter bore necessary for the crown nut. Finish everything with a waterproof finish such as polyurethane varnish. I prefer no finish at all on the inside where food contact will be, but

there are a number of nontoxic finishes if you wish.

A Gift for a King's Cook

Install the mechanism and we now have a gift to warm the heart of any cook. You may even get a good meal out of the endeavour. A final note according to *Gourmet Magazine*. It is the fresh ground nature that a pepper mill imparts to the spice. Otherwise all peppercorns are equal so find the cheapest bulk source you can. Paying a higher price for pepper will only be squandering your hard turned cash. ∎

Maurice Mullins' love of wood, and interest in it, is lifelong. Two years studying at art school, ten years as an engineer/technologist and eight years working in forestry and timber conversion culminated in 1982 with the decision to make woodturning a full-time business.

Being up to this time largely self-taught, he says 'I decided to formalize my decision by completing a Start Your Own Business Course followed by one year on the Manpower Services Commission's Enterprise Scheme.

The award in 1985 of a Northern Arts equipment grant of £900 enabled him to update his lathe equipment and considerably boosted his confidence/morale.

In 1987 he obtained a credit in the Open University Course *'Design, Products and Processes'*, and in the same year exhibited at the Harrogate (Trade) Crafts Show. This established the bread and butter side of his business.

In 1988 the award of a Northern Arts personal development grant enabled him to attend the opening of the International Turned Objects Show (in which a set of his goblets appeared) and also the third seminar of the American Association of Woodturners.

He exhibited at Loughborough in 1989 and demonstrated there in 1991. His many other notable appearances include a six-week residency at Grizedale Forest in 1990 where he worked alongside Merryll Saylan in demonstrating lathe skills.

Love Goblet with Integral Ring

MAURICE MULLINS

If you missed it at Loughborough, here is a re-run of a demonstration that attracted a large and appreciative audience.

I can clearly remember the first time I made a small goblet with a ring around its stem. I had decided to try and make a living from woodturning which I previously enjoyed as a hobby (happy days!) . . . Well it must have been six or more years ago that I drove across to Blythe in Northumberland to visit Alan Batty, primarily to look at a lathe which was high up on my short list of possibles. Alan as usual was very helpful. He ably demonstrated the lathe but I was put off buying that particular model because of the messing around with a spanner to move the tool rest.

What did impress and fascinate me was a small goblet in yew with a tiny ring around its slender stem which Alan had made. It was almost 50mm 2" high and of good proportions. You can easily guess what I made on my lathe as soon as I got home — Yes! you're right . . . a pile of broken goblets!

Over the years, I have developed my own techniques to the point where I now make and sell various $\frac{1}{12}$" scale objects as part of my bread and butter work. A couple of years ago I saw Alan who was then working in Yorkshire. I showed him some of my goblets with rings, less than 12mm $\frac{1}{2}$" high and he seemed impressed and pleased that his work had resulted in a challenge for me. I hope it will also be a challenge for you — you never know where it might take you! I had a set of goblets selected for ITOS (International Turned Objects Show) which resulted in a woodturning trip to America!

Woods

However, let's begin to make a goblet of a more workable size from 75mm 3" to 125mm 5" high. A thin wall and a thin stem means that the most suitable woods are dense and close grained; I have made goblets out of all kinds of woods and find holly, cherry, laburnum, damson, apple, etc. satisfactory but my favourite is English yew. Irish yew tends to have more knots which can cause problems when getting down to a stem less than 3mm diameter. The wood ideally can be freshly cut or partially dry, the former being easier to cut.

For any lathe work where bark is present it is essential to wear a full face mask. A blank complete with bark is cut to a length of 120mm 4¾" approx (Photo 1) mounted between centres and a 40mm x 4mm 1⅝" x ⅛" spigot is cut to fit my

Photo 1

Photo 2

collet chuck. (Photo 2.) Fit the blank into the chuck and tighten securely. Usually I first take a cut across the bowl and, if necessary, remove most of the bark, leaving about 25mm 1" of bark remaining around the bowl area. This will reduce

Photo 3

possible vibrations to a minimum. With a gouge well over on its side I can hollow out the bowl, taking great care when cutting the bark (Photo 3). The tool must be fed in very slowly and at precisely the right angle as the bevel of the gouge cannot be used effectively to control the cut until it is in the continual wall of the bowl itself. It might be a good idea to practise the bowl forming cuts before attemping to make a complete goblet in one go. I have had, and still do get, the odd disaster at this stage, so don't give up! If necessary a very light cut with a freshly sharpened round nose scraper, followed by the finish of your choice, completes the inside of the bowl. I personally use wet and dry sandpaper lubricated with sunflower oil but you could use Melamine finish if you prefer a high gloss finish.

Outside Shape

(Photo 4) The outside shape of the bowl is now cut using a sharp gouge, again well over on its side. To measure the thick-

Photo 4

ness of the cup as I cut, I tend to rely on feel by carefully using my thumb and second finger as a calliper whilst the work is revolving, but you can stop the lathe easily and use the same method. You might like to try shining a light through the bowl wall but, through practice, I've become quite good at telling the wall thickness by feel and seldom use the other methods.

Thickness

How thick or thin should the

wall be? It's up to you. Whatever your nerves will stand! On a goblet of this size I would be aiming at a rim wall thickness of about 1mm to 1.5mm gradually rising to a maximum of 2mm as you near the stem. It's all a question of proportion. What looks right and what doesn't! A thick bowl on a thin stem will not, to me, look balanced.

Once you have reached the stage shown in Photo 5 you can sand and finish before bringing in some support help. This comes in the form of a revolving dead centre which has been

Photo 5

fitted with a small wooden plug. On to the plug I have dolloped a quantity of glue from a glue gun. Just before the glue has set, I cover the inside of the cup with some cling film and

carefully advance the revolving dead centre into the cup. (The glue forms a perfect fit with the inside of the bowl and should not stick as the cling film should prevent this.) Remember, this is a support only, so do not exert any force on the work. Once made, this support chuck can be re-used several times before a fresh blob of glue will be required. (Photo 6.)

Ring

The next step is to cut the ring.

Photo 6

This starts life as a disc. I choose a place to cut the disc which is free of knots and other blemishes. (Photo 7.) To round off the outer ring I use a specially ground scraper as shown in sketch 8. (Photo 8.)

I cut from one side, then the other, as shown, and end up

Photo 7

Photo 8

with a perfect outside shape. To sharpen the scraper, I use a high speed drill fitted with a

Photo 9

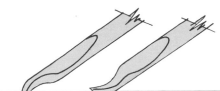

small cone-shaped grinding wheel. (Photo 9.) This stone is also used to keep the hook tools that form the inside shape of the ring in good condition. (See sketch.) I make my hook tool from worn out HSS gouges (Photo 10.) although you can

Photo 10

use the tang of a small file bent to shape and ground but it does not last long because of the heat build up during the cut. Each hook tool is designed to cut one side only.

At this stage do not cut through (Photo 11). Cut as much of the

Photo 11

Photo 12

ring as you can, then sand and polish. Gently cut through from each side to release the ring (Photo 12). The stem and base are now created (Photo 13). Again, keep looking for a sense

Photo 13

of proportion — the base should be no smaller than the outside of the ring. And the base needs to be considerably smaller than the cup otherwise it will look base heavy.

Stem

To cut the thin stem, I start from the cup end and work towards the base using a 12mm ½″ gouge on its side (Photo 14). I know it's not done to drag the gouge uphill towards the base but I find it does work — in effect you are using the gouge as a skew chisel.

The base is defined and the

Photo 14

Photo 15

stem cut to the desired diameter (Photo 15) . . . don't try to go too thin at first or you can become very frustrated. I have cut away part of my short tool rest to allow my long fingers to reach and support delicate work of this nature. I can now smooth off the inside of the ring. In this case, I have glued a 10mm ⅜″ strip of wet and dry sandpaper to a 6mm ¼″ dowel which has been cut and sanded to give a semi-circular section from the handle to its tip. Next, sand and polish the whole goblet before parting off — be gentle!

180 grit wet/dry paper is glued onto semi circular section of the 6mm ø ¼″ dowel

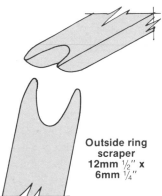

Left hand inside scraper 6mm ø ¼″ **Right hand inside scraper 6mm ø ¼″**

Outside ring scraper 12mm ½″ x 6mm ¼″

Warning

A word of warning at this stage. If you have to stop the lathe for any reason, BEWARE! **When you switch the lathe off, do not use any method of braking, i.e. let the lathe slow down until it stops of its own accord.** And when you restart, remember the collet chuck accelerates quickly to its running speed but the inertia of the tailstock revolving centre at rest is only overcome by a 3mm ⅛″ diameter wooden shaft that is not really strong enough to cope with the shock twisting motion. To reduce the chances of a twisted stem you can reduce the lathe speed and start turning the collet chuck by hand, and then switch on once the chuck is moving.

Conical-shaped grinding wheel for use in a high speed drill such as a Dremel. The cone shape ensures a clearance angle all around the cutting edge.

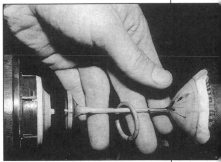

I recently demonstrated how to make these goblets at the last Loughborough Symposium and I was rather spoilt as the 'lads' from LRE Machinery had kindly supplied, for demonstration purposes, a Canadian 'General' lathe fitted with a variable speed control. This proved to be excellent for this type of work as the work piece could be started from rest slowly up to working speed just by turning a small knob. (Please, Father Christmas!)

Parting Off

To part off the base, I use 3mm ⅛″ parting off tool (Photo 15) fed in at a slight angle so that ultimately the cup will stand on the rim of its base.

Photo 16

I normally part off completely leaving a nib about 3mm ⅛″ diameter but I would suggest that for first attempts you play safe. Stop the lathe and saw through the last few millimetres. You may find that the goblet seems to be firmly stuck to the tailstock chuck (Photo 16). Just be patient and slowly bend the goblet to release the vacuum seal. Remove the nib with a sharp chisel or small sanding disc — and there is your finished goblet! . . . You could also try making a goblet 50mm 2″ long, then 25mm 1″ long, then 12mm ½″ long. It can be done . . . or perhaps you prefer to wait for my next article on making miniature goblets. Keep on practising!

One thing I have learnt from this exercise is that it is very difficult taking photographs at the same time as you are turning! ∎

Bonnie Klein has been turning for a hobby since 1975. She began to get more serious in the early 1980s and then started her business, Klein Design of Renton, Washington, several years ago.

The business consists of producing and making her 'mini bowl lathe', the Klein Design Short Bed Lathe (available in England from Craft Supplies Ltd, Buxton), making turnings to sell and teaching turning classes. She demonstrates frequently for clubs and tool shops and at conferences and woodworking shows throughout America and abroad. She loves all aspects of the business but regrets the shortage of time.

'My love of wood and tools,' she says, 'began at an early age. My father is a builder and always was supportive of projects I had in mind. My mother didn't believe in having a TV in the house, but kept my sister and me very busy with books and making things with our hands. There were always new crafts to explore. I have raised two children, a boy and a girl, and can now devote most of my time and energy to the business.

**Bonnie Klein
Klein Design
17910 SE 110th Street
Renton, WA. 98059
USA**

Several years ago, in an antique store, I found an old turned ivory box with a lid that could be unscrewed. I was fascinated and became determined to learn how to make containers with threaded lids. I talked to a couple of machinists and read through every magazine article and book that I could find that had any information about threads. After figuring out what was needed I started to gather the parts.

Building the Threading Jig

Basically, the jig consists of a spinning cutter bit held in a flexible shaft handpiece. The workpiece is advanced past it while being held on the end of a threaded rod guided by a set of nuts of the desired thread pitch. (Photo A.)

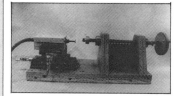

A The workpiece held on the end of a threaded rod

I had a machinist make the threaded rod, also known as a 'lead screw', about 460mm 18" long with a section at the front end the same size as the spindle of my lathe — 20mm ¾" — 16 tpi, on which to mount my chucks. It is important that the chucks are able to tighten up against a 'true' surface, so the machinist turned a flange 15mm ⅝" thick x 38mm 1½" in diameter (photo B) between the

B The turned flange

Making a Box with a Threaded Lid

BONNIE KLEIN

The author's boxes, like her miniatures, are admired by woodturners throughout the world. Here, in words and pictures, is a step-by-step account of how she makes them.

spindle threads and the rest of the rod threads which determine the amount of threads per inch you will get in your workpiece. In my opinion 16-20 tpi would work well for most projects. I chose to use 16 tpi.

The next item I obtained was a cutter bit that is described in a catalogue as a 'double angle 12mm ½" shank, cobalt cutter with a 60° included angle'. I had to have a machinist reduce the 12mm ½" shank down to 6mm ¼" to fit the tool I chose to use. I am able to use this one cutter bit to cut both the inside and the outside threads. There

are other cutter bits available with 3mm ⅛" shafts but I feel the 6mm ¼" is important for stability.

There are several tools which could be used to drive the cutter bit, such as a die grinder, router or Dremel Moto tool. I chose to use a Foredom tool, with a flexible shaft handpiece, which turns the bit at 20,000 rpm. It doesn't take much power to cut these small threads, but I feel they are cut cleaner with the higher speed.

An adjustable device could be home-built to hold the cutting tool but I decided to use what is called a 'cross slide vise', also known as an x-y vise, available through a tool company or catalogue. (Photo C.) Mounted at the proper height, it has the capability of moving the cutting tool laterally or longtitudinally, very precisely, simply and quickly. I used two blocks of wood with long vee grooves to hold the handpiece between the jaws of the vise. **(We checked with Bonnie Klein who confirmed that the cutter runs vertically. She adds that, as the threads are 16 per inch and the diameter of the cutter is so small, the cutting angle does not appear to be critical. But maybe if a coarser thread and larger cutter were used then a slight adjustment to the angle should be considered. — Ed.)**

C The cross slide vise

For rigidity, I selected a 50mm 2″ thick piece of wood, 200mm 8″ x 610mm 24″ as the base for the threading jig, and mounted the cross-slide vise on the left side. I built the support frame for the 'lead screw' on the right side so that the horizontal centre line is the same height as the centre line of the cutter bit.

The vertical supports are approximately 200mm 8″ apart for stability. The lead screw is guided through the vertical supports by two large nuts made by the machinist. (Photo D.) These can be 'loaded'

D Two large nuts guide the lead screw through the vertical supports

by tightening towards each other before securely fastening them to the support frame. By doing this, the backlash, which is important for thread accuracy, can be taken out of the lead screw. I turned a wooden disc to use as a crank handle for the right hand end of the head screw for advancing it toward the cutter.

Turning of the boxes takes place on the lathe, but when the piece is ready for the threads, the chuck with the workpiece in it is taken to the jig, the threads are cut, then they are returned to the lathe for final turning.

Threading the Box

For a small box start with a cylinder of wood about 50mm 2″ in diameter and 63mm 2½″ long, with the grain running lengthwise or from top to bottom through the finished piece. Usually there will be less distortion of the lid fit with the grain in this direction. I make my threaded boxes in a 3 Jaw chuck because it is the most accurate chuck I have for moving back and forth between the lathe and the threaded jig.

Mount the cylinder in the chuck, with the lid end toward the headstock, then true up the face and as much of the sides as can be reached. Determine the proportion of the lid to the base and, allowing for the width of the parting cut, separate the base from the lid. It is good practice to label the bottom of the base so it can be mounted in the chuck correctly, ensuring that the grain will be aligned in the finished piece. (Photo 1.)

Working on the lid section still in the chuck, clean up the parting cut by removing a minimum amount of wood. (The more wood that is removed in this area, the less chance for a good grain match in the finished piece.) After shaping the inside of the lid, an area is cut straight and parallel for the inside threads. This should be a minimum length equal to the width of four threads, preferably five or six threads.

1 It is good practice to label the bottom of the base

2 Cutting a bevel where the first thread is to be cut

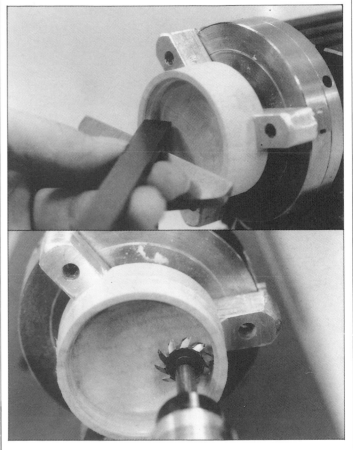

3 The teeth on the cutter bit should just brush the area to be threaded

A clearance cut needs to be made in one of two places, either at the beginning of the female threads or after the last of the male threads. I prefer to make it at the beginning of the female threads because, not only is it easier to cut, but it will also aid in centring the lid on the base. This is easily done by cutting a step at the inside edge of the lid the width and depth of at least one thread. Cut a bevel where the first thread is to be cut. The bevel prevents your having a very thin thread at the beginning. (Photo 2.)

I have found that by flowing some of the thin variety of the cyanoacrylate glue over the area to be threaded it soaks into the fibres a bit and helps to strengthen the threads. Sanding and finishing the inside of the lid is done at this time.

Remove the chuck, with the workpiece still in it, from the lathe and screw it onto the threading jig lead screw right up tight to the flange. Adjust the lead screw and the cutting tool so the teeth on the cutter bit just brush the area to be threaded. (Photo 3.) Back the lead screw off so the work is out of the way and advance the cutter bit laterally, toward the outside of the box, just enough to cut a depth of thread that will leave very, very tiny flats remaining on the tips. (Photo 4.) The markings on the vise will be helpful in determining how deep this is, and are useful for repeated projects because it will be the same each time. (Photo 5.)

4 The depth of thread

backing it off. The hardness of the wood determines how fast to advance the lead screw. On some woods, if the piece isn't advanced quickly enough, the cutter will leave burn marks. (Photo 6.)

6 Hardness of the wood determines how fast to advance the lead screw

Return the chuck, with the lid still mounted in it, to the lathe and very lightly sand the threaded area. I prefer not to put a finish on the threads, because any moisture in the finish will tend to expand the fibres and some finishes may make the threaded area sticky. A little wax is helpful on some woods but take care not to do anything to interfere with the fit. The lid section may now be

removed from the chuck. It is good practice to mark one of the jaws, and the location of the workpiece, before removing it, just in case it might be necessary to put it back into the chuck.

Mount the base in the chuck with the bottom toward the headstock. True the sides and face taking care not to remove any more wood than is absolutely necessary from the face. Measure the diameter of the threaded area inside the lid (Photo 7) and add enough to

7 Measuring the diameter of the threaded area

8 Cut the tenon on the base slightly larger than needed

9 Dial calipers

allow for the meshing of the threads. Cut the tenon on the base slightly larger in diameter than needed. (Photo 8.) This will give an idea of wall thickness possibilities. The actual size will be determined, and the threads will be cut, after the interior of the base is finished because occasionally the shapes will change due to the relieving of stresses in the wood. Completely sand and finish the interior of the box.

Leaving a shoulder, a tenon is cut (Photo 9) larger in diameter

than the female threads by adding slightly less than twice the depth of a thread. Once this difference is established, it should be the same for other boxes using the same thread pitch. I use dial calipers to obtain this measurement. After determining the diameter, it is necessary to cut the tenon to the proper length. I like the lid to screw onto the base in about one and a half revolutions. In one of my early boxes the lid turned almost four revolutions before coming off, making it obvious to me that it was a situation to be avoided. I have determined that a tenon length a little less than the width of three threads works well. As before, cut a bevel where the threads are to begin, to avoid having a very thin thread. (Photo 10.)

10 Taking care to avoid having a very thin thread

Before taking the chuck and workpiece to the threading jig, flow a little of the very thin cyanoacrylate glue over the area to be threaded to add strength to the fibres. With the chuck now on the spindle of the lead screw, the adjustments are made to bring the cutter teeth to the point of just brushing the surface of the area to be threaded. (Photo 11.) The workpiece is backed out of the way and the cutter advanced laterally into the area of the box the same amount as for the thread depth on the lid. The threads are then cut by advancing the lead screw as before. (Photo 12.)

5 Markings on the vise

The threads are usually cut in one pass but sometimes there is a need to go back and cut them just a little bit deeper. Cut a minimum of about three or four revolutions because it is preferable to have too many threads than not enough in the lid. It is better to cut in only one direction — on the advance of the lead screw — not while

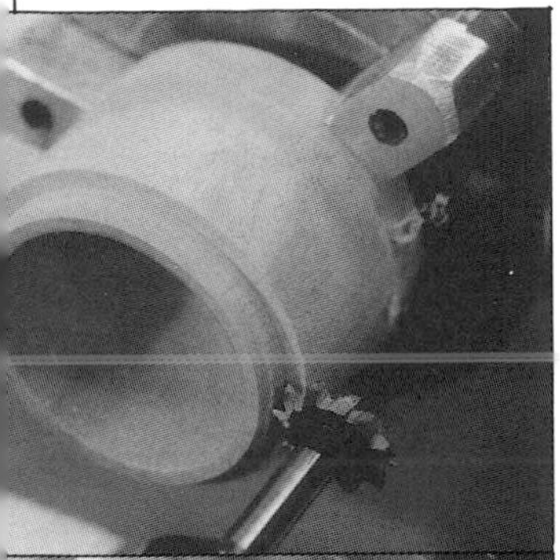

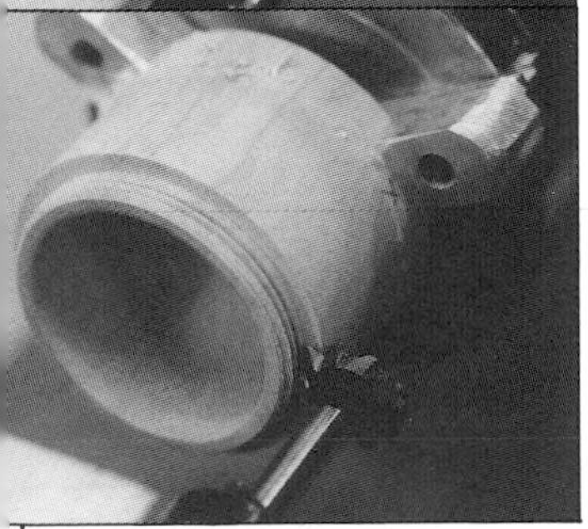

11 The cutter teeth just brush the surface

12 Advancing the lead screw

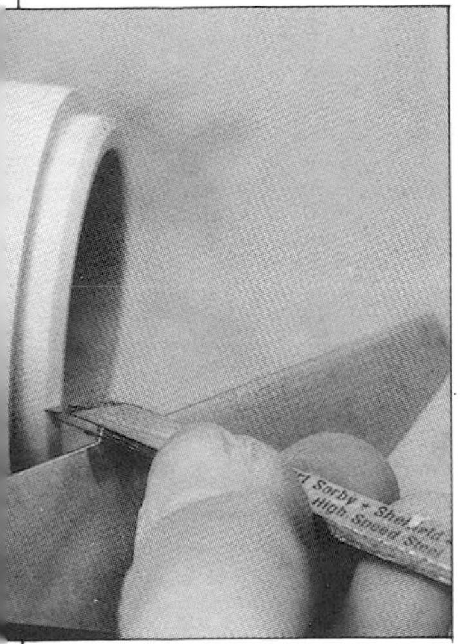

It usually takes about two revolutions before it becomes necessary to stop to avoid cutting into the shoulder.

Check the fit of the lid by either backing the lead screw off and out of the way or by removing the cutting tool laterally, **but not until a note is made of the location of the cutter bit just in case the threads aren't deep enough. Avoid moving the cutter bit longtitudinally because that will change the location of the thread grooves and it may be difficult to get it lined up exactly for another pass.**

When the desired fit is achieved it is time to return the chuck and workpiece to the lathe. The threads are then lightly sanded and the lid is screwed onto the base. Now the exterior of the lid, and most of the sides of the box, can be turned to the final shape. Then the adjustments can be made that will bring the grain into alignment. This is done by reducing, ever so carefully, the shoulder that the lid is coming down against. It is best to stop just a little short of the perfect alignment (Photo 13) because, after removing and replacing the lid several times, the threads will wear some and the grain match will change. The outside of the lid and most of the sides can be sanded and finished. (Photo 14.)

13 Stopping just a little short of the perfect alignment

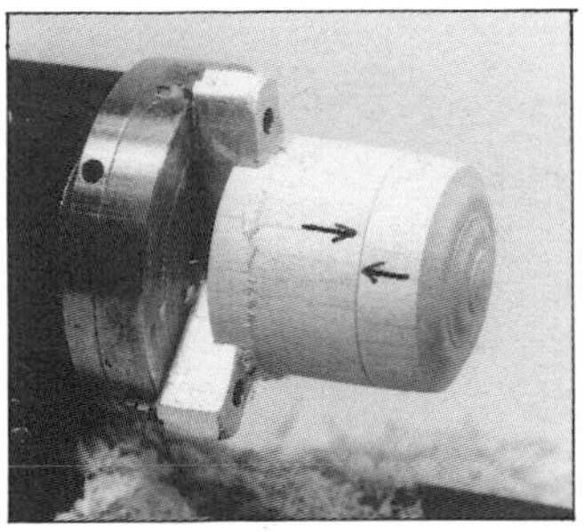

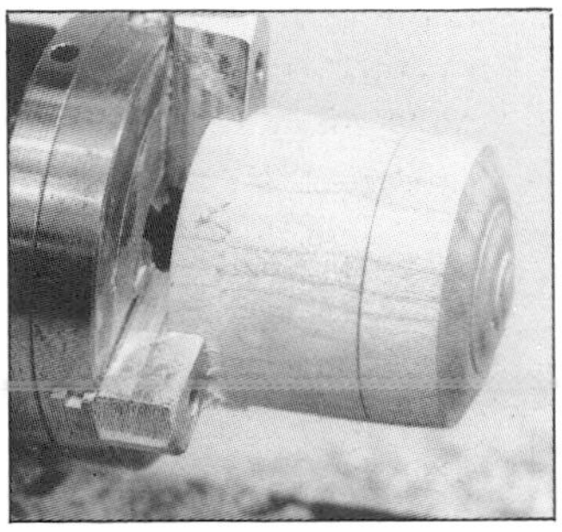

14 Grain in alignment

Now the base of the box may be removed from the chuck in preparation for finishing the bottom. With a waste block mounted on a face plate, make a jam fit chuck by turning a tenon approximately 6mm ¼" long (Photo 15) for the box base to fit onto. (Photo 16.) The bottom and the rest of the sides are then turned, detailed, sanded and finished. (Photo 17.)

15 Turning a ¼" long tenon

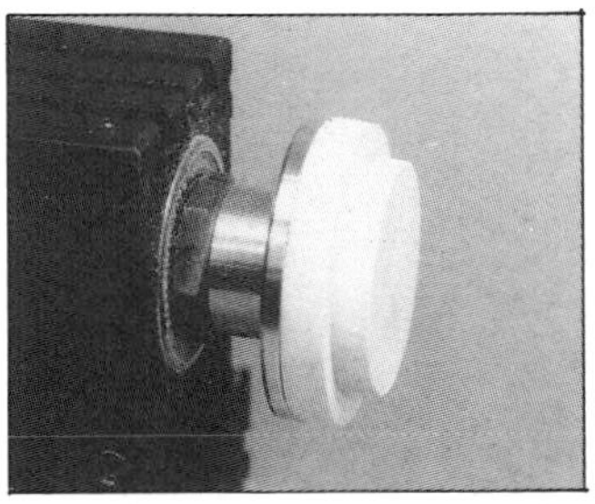

A few other boxes by Bonnie

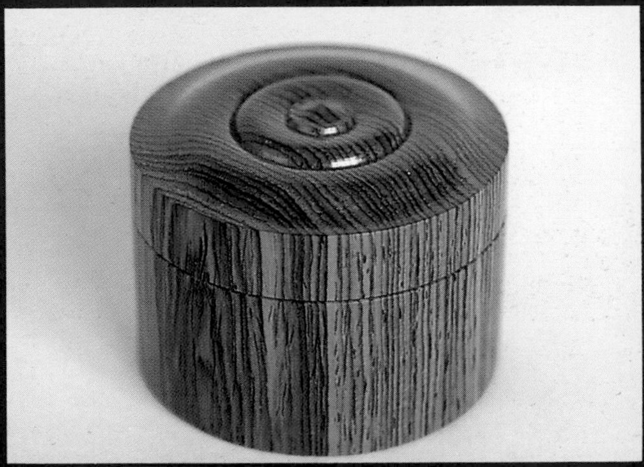

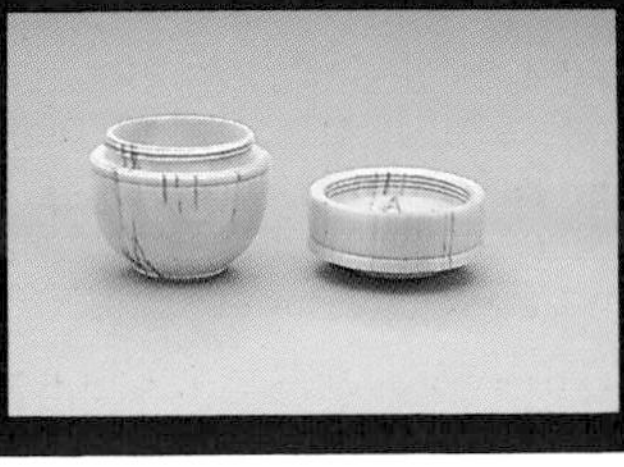

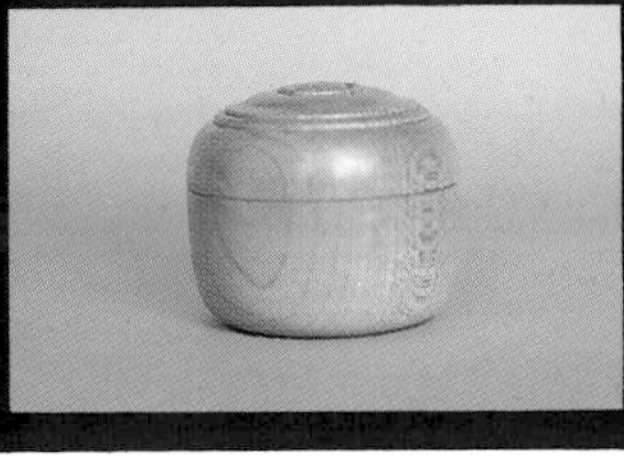

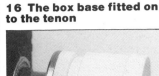

16 The box base fitted on to the tenon

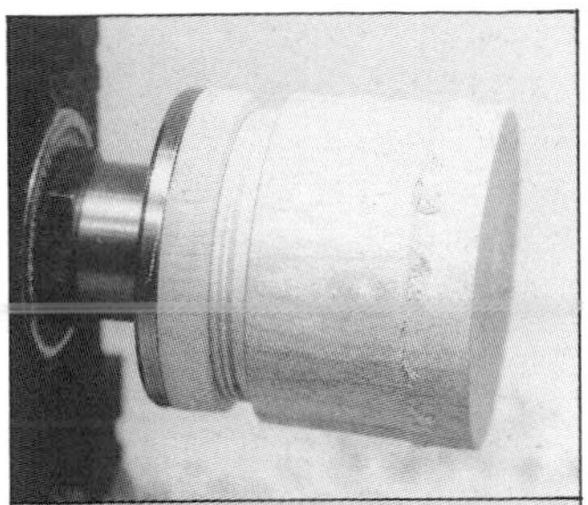

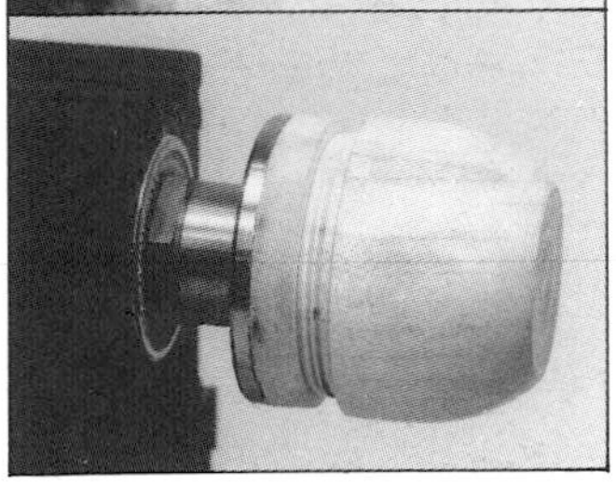

17 The bottom and sides turned, detailed, sanded and finished

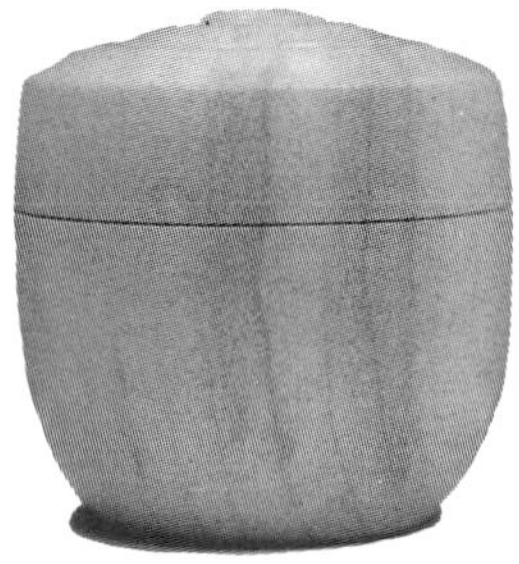

18 The finished box

Screw the lid on and admire your box. (Photo 18.)

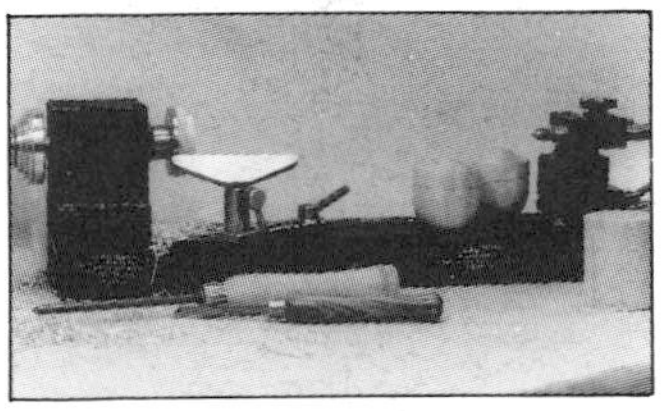

19 The lathe used — Bonnie's own 'mini bowl lathe' which she developed for ease of use over the bed ways

In conclusion, I would like to point out that this is only one way of creating a box with a threaded lid. There are many possible variations in the jig as well as the construction details and design elements of the container. For instance, the lid could thread inside instead of over the base, the box exterior doesn't have to be turned or the material could be something other than wood. Use these ideas to spark your own creativity! ■

Chris Pye has been both a professional woodturner and carver over some 16 years. He started with carving, owing his formative introduction to the master woodcarver Gino Masero, and a little later added woodturning.

He considers himself self taught, and equally at home in both crafts, often combining them.

Chris was born in Co. Durham but has lived a large part of his life in the South West of England and currently lives in Bristol.

His carvings are mainly commissioned, and range from lettering and heraldry, figurework and personal sculpture to the restoration of old carvings.

His turned work includes newel posts (up to 2.9 metres 9′ 6″ long), stair parts, table legs, lamps and knobs for the trade as well as individual bowls and boxes.

Turning and carving are combined in four poster bedposts, barley twists, lettered bowls, columns and one-off pieces.

He has several years' experience teaching adult education classes in woodcarving as well as private students in both turning and carving. In 1990 he demonstrated at the AWGB Seminar at Loughborough. At present he is writing the first of a series of books around the area of carving and turning.

Chris is a Buddhist and is married with two children.
Chris Pye
The Poplars
Ewyas Harold
Hereford
HR2 OHU

GET A HANDLE

Photo 1 Handles from various carving tools showing different sizes, shapes and woods.

CHRIS PYE

Having turned a mallet from a bowls wood on pages 60–63 Chris now looks at making and fitting some handles to hit with it.

In the previous article we made my friend's mallet from a bowls wood. Now I am going to make a chisel handle.

Like the mallet, although straightforward, there is more to this project than meets the eye. It seems best to begin by describing those features that make a good chisel or gouge handle, which help us as we use it. We will see where problems might lie.

Photo 1 shows the handles of just a small sample of the many carving tools I use in my work. Only when mass-produced is there a standard shape and size tool handle.

Carvers do have a tradition of making their own handles from available scraps of wood, often making them octagonal so they didn't roll about on the bench.

It's a good idea to make handles from different woods and in different shapes to allow easy identification. If ever you tackle carving proper you may have 40 tools out on a bench full of chippings. Different shapes, sizes and wood colours help the eye sort them out.

The tang is the part of the tool that inserts into the handle. It is usually tapered and square in section, but can look like a square or round rod, not tapering at all. The particular chisel in this project has a parallel square tang, but I will be including the other types as well (FIG 1).

The handle needs to fit well and securely, along the axis of

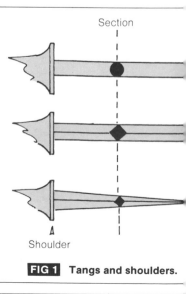

Section

Shoulder

FIG 1 Tangs and shoulders.

N YOUR TOOLS

the blade. This implies a straight tang, which, unfortunately, is not always the case.

A tool with an offset tang, producing a degree of bend at the handle, can end up bending more when subject to heavy mallet work. As the tang is annealed metal you can address this problem with a hammer and file.

While you are checking the tang, make sure the shoulder has a flat face to meet the wood of the handle.

The handle is, quite literally, an extension of the hand, and an edge tool handles better if the blade lines up correctly and sits firmly.

Holes for tangs: For a parallel round tang make the hole an exact tight fit along the length of the tang.

For a parallel square tang bore the hole a size halfway between the diagonal of the square and one of its sides (FIG 2). The corners of the tang bite into the wood of the hole.

For a tapered tang bore one guiding pilot hole about 3mm ⅛" DIA and use the twist method of fitting the handle which is described later.

If the wood is something like box, with a propensity for splitting, consider a second hole bored in about a third of the length of the first hole. Take a measurement of the diagonal of the tapering tang at about one third from the shoulder and make this the diameter of the second hole.

Ferrules. Usually of brass, these are needed where there is a danger of the wood splitting. Small tools with good wood and, especially, with a shoulder can get away without them.

If you can't get the real thing look to brass, copper, steel tubing etc. with reasonably thin walls. Although not obligatory, a bevel filed on the inside edge of one end of such tube makes for the tightest fit when it is squeezed onto the wood of the handle.

Shapes of some handles are suggested in FIG 3. My friend had very firm ideas about what he wanted, so in this case we are making quite a fat, barrel shape.

The main point about shape is comfort. You can vary the shape by varying the length and width, the overall shape, where the belly or maximum width of

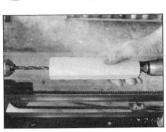
Photo 2 Boring the hole for the tang.

Photo 3 Tail centre into hole around which the shape will be turned.

Photo 4 Sizing down to the outside diameter of the ferrule.

any barrel shape is in relation to the length, and the number and position of grip grooves.

Wood. Straight-grained, resilient hardwood is needed. Ash, hickory, beech and box have always been favourites.

If you are making a handle for a smaller chisel or gouge, one that will not be hit with a mallet, or perhaps only lightly, then many other woods such as yew, walnut, rosewood or maple can be used. The wood used in the demonstration is ash.

Start with a square sectioned piece of wood. This need only be accurately bandsawn, cutting the wood about 25mm 1" longer than the final handle length and a little over the maximum thickness required. Mark the centres at each end and take the corners off on the bandsaw.

Tools and Equipment. I used the following: 25mm 1" roughing gouge, 32mm 1¼" skew chisel, 10mm ⅜" square chisel, 4 prong drive centre and revolving tail centre, Jacobs chuck with twist bits to suit, callipers, sandpaper and sealer.

Method. The hole is bored first and the handle turned around the hole. In this way the hole lines up along the handle, axially. How the hole is bored depends on the shape of the tang — see the note on this above. ▶

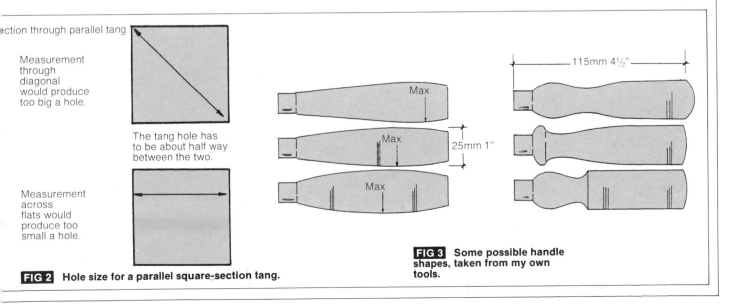

ction through parallel tang

Measurement through diagonal would produce too big a hole.

The tang hole has to be about half way between the two.

Measurement across flats would produce too small a hole.

FIG 2 Hole size for a parallel square-section tang.

Max

Max

Max

25mm 1"

115mm 4½"

FIG 3 Some possible handle shapes, taken from my own tools.

So with the Jacobs chuck and bit in the drive end of the lathe, and revolving at a slow speed, feed the wood from the tailstock to the necessary depth. The drill bit depth can be marked with masking tape (Photo 2).

Remove the wood and Jacobs chuck from the lathe and fit the normal drive centre. Reverse the wood onto the lathe so the point of the revolving centre is in the hole and tighten up (Photo 3).

Rough the handle to a cylinder and move in the tool rest as close as possible.

Fit the ferrule next. Mark its length and a little extra onto the end of the wood.

Using the square chisel and callipers come down carefully to the outside diameter of the ferrule (Photo 4). Keep the shoulder square.

The final fitting is best done by a softly, softly method of trial and error. Stop the lathe and try pushing on the ferrule.

Remember to offer the bevel end to the wood. Creep up on a final diameter where the ferrule pushes on tightly.

You may need to take the handle off the lathe and, with the ferrule on the edges of a vice, tap it home.

> 'Only when mass-produced is there a standard shape and size tool handle.'

Now, with the ferrule in place, the handle can be shaped as you wish. Round the end away from the ferrule so that it doesn't dig into the hand when you are using the chisel.

Don't run the wood completely down to the ferrule but leave it a little proud where they meet. A definite, but small, shoulder remains.

Sand and seal with, say, a coat of cellulose lacquer, cut back finely. Burnish with shavings. Don't make the surface shiny or slippy with a glossy finish as this makes the grip uncomfortable.

Use the point of the skew chisel to trim back the excess wood at the ferrule end, but take care not to go through to the metal of the revolving centre (Photo 5).

Remove the handle from the lathe and, holding it in a vice, finish off both ends with a chisel and sandpaper. Make sure the wood is flat where it will fit the shoulder of the chisel. Seal the ends as before.

Finally punch a depression on each side of the ferrule. A

Photo 5 Cleaning off excess wood beyond the ferrule with the skew chisel. Make sure you have a flat surface on which to seat the shoulder of the blade.

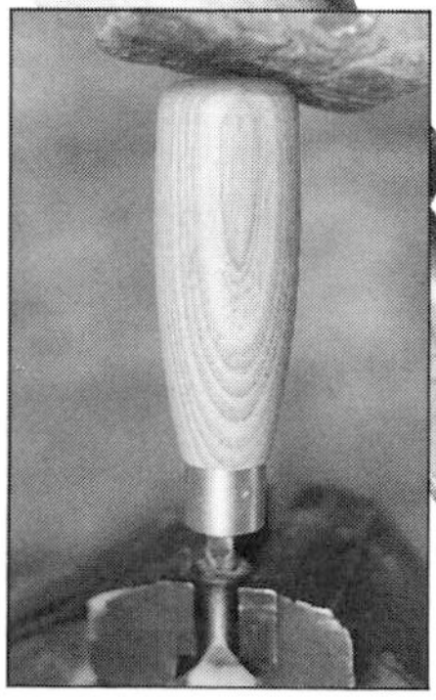

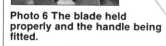

Photo 6 The blade held properly and the handle being fitted.

nail will do for this. Should the wood shrink this acts to hold the ferrule in place.

Fitting the handle. For this it's best to use a metalworking vice with metal linings. If you don't have one and are using a woodworking vice, protect any wooden linings with scrap hardwood.

Grip the chisel by the blade so that the shoulder is supported on the jaws of the vice and the tang points straight up in the air. It is especially important, when thumping on a handle, to hold the blade properly, as I learned, the hard way.

If you set the tool upright with the cutting end on a resistant surface there is a danger of cracking the tool. The pressures have nowhere to go when you thump it. The other trick is not to thump it too hard!

If the holes are the right size, the parallel tangs, both round and square, should knock straight on with a mallet.

With a tapered tang proceed as follows: Tap the handle, with its pilot hole, onto the tang a little way then twist it around a little. You are using the tang to ream out the hole.

Tap the handle a little more and twist it again. Keep repeating this process with the handle in one hand and the mallet in the other, taking the handle off now and then to clear the dust by tapping it (Photo 6).

You will fairly quickly get the rhythm and before long will have set the handle down on the tang to within 3mm ⅛' of the shoulder.

At this point clear the dust out one last time and select which part of the handle, perhaps a pleasing bit of grain, you want and where. Now you can tap the handle home and there should be no problem of splitting.

If your tang and holes are true the blade will be aligned along the axis of the handle.

One point — the method by which the tang is heated and burnt into the handle would be appropriate only if you could not bore a hole and you were really desperate! While I'm sure it's great fun, it charcoals the wood inside, allowing the handle to work loose.

It can also be messy and not without its dangers, both to your lungs and a wood workshop. It can, if you are not careful, damage the tool tempering, and it is much slower than anything described here.

And that's it. My friend now has a working chisel to go with the mallet (Photo 7) and needs only to set off in search of something to communicate with. ∎

Photo 7 The mallet and chisel handle.

BIBLIOGRAPHY

Works referred to in this book

ROWLEY, Keith. *Woodturning: A Foundation Course*, GMC Publications, 1990

JACOBSON, Edward. *The Art of Turned-Wood Bowls*, E P Dutton Inc, USA, 1985

NISH, Dale. *Master Woodturners*, Artisan Press, USA, 1985

PINTO, Edward H. *Treen and Other Wooden Bygones: An Encyclopaedia and Social History*, Bell & Hyman, London 1969

HOPPER, Ray. *Multi-Centre Woodturning*, GMC Publications, 1992

INDEX

INDEX (continued)

WOODTURNING

Adventures in Woodturning	David Springett	Pleasure & Profit from Woodturning	Reg Sherwin
Bert Marsh: Woodturner	Bert Marsh	Practical Tips for Turners & Carvers	GMC Publications
Bill Jones' Notes from the Turning Shop	Bill Jones	Practical Tips for Woodturners	GMC Publications
Carving on Turning	Chris Pye	Spindle Turning	GMC Publications
Colouring Techniques for Woodturners	Jan Sanders	Turning Miniatures in Wood	John Sainsbury
Decorative Techniques for Woodturners	Hilary Bowen	Turning Wooden Toys	Terry Lawrence
Faceplate Turning: Features, Projects, Practice	GMC Publications	Useful Woodturning Projects	GMC Publications
Green Woodwork	Mike Abbott	Woodturning: A Foundation Course	Keith Rowley
Illustrated Woodturning Techniques	John Hunnex	Woodturning Jewellery	Hilary Bowen
Keith Rowley's Woodturning Projects	Keith Rowley	Woodturning Masterclass	Tony Boase
Make Money from Woodturning	Ann & Bob Phillips	Woodturning: A Source Book of Shapes	John Hunnex
Multi-Centre Woodturning	Ray Hopper	Woodturning Techniques	GMC Publications
		Woodturning Wizardry	David Springett

WOODCARVING

The Art of the Woodcarver	GMC Publications	Wildfowl Carving Volume 1	Jim Pearce
Carving Birds & Beasts	GMC Publications	Wildfowl Carving Volume 2	Jim Pearce
Carving Realistic Birds	David Tippey	Woodcarving: A Complete Course	Ron Butterfield
Carving on Turning	Chris Pye	Woodcarving for Beginners: Projects, Techniques & Tools	
Decorative Woodcarving	Jeremy Williams		GMC Publications
Practical Tips for Turners & Carvers	GMC Publications	Woodcarving Tools, Materials & Equipment	Chris Pye

PLANS, PROJECTS, TOOLS & THE WORKSHOP

40 More Woodworking Plans & Projects	GMC Publications	Sharpening: The Complete Guide	Jim Kingshott
Electric Woodwork: Power Tool Woodworking	Jeremy Broun	Sharpening Pocket Reference Book	Jim Kingshott
The Incredible Router	Jeremy Broun	Woodworking Plans & Projects	GMC Publications
Making & Modifying Woodworking Tools	Jim Kingshott	The Workshop	Jim Kingshott

TOYS & MINIATURES

Designing & Making Wooden Toys	Terry Kelly	Making Wooden Toys & Games	Jeff & Jennie Loader
Heraldic Miniature Knights	Peter Greenhill	Miniature Needlepoint Carpets	Janet Granger
Making Board, Peg & Dice Games	Jeff & Jennie Loader	Restoring Rocking Horses	Clive Green & Anthony Dew
Making Little Boxes from Wood	John Bennett	Turning Miniatures in Wood	John Sainsbury
Making Unusual Miniatures	Graham Spalding	Turning Wooden Toys	Terry Lawrence

CREATIVE CRAFTS

The Complete Pyrography	Stephen Poole	Creating Knitwear Designs	Pat Ashforth & Steve Plummer
Cross Stitch on Colour	Sheena Rogers	Making Knitwear Fit	Pat Ashforth & Steve Plummer
Embroidery Tips & Hints	Harold Hayes	Miniature Needlepoint Carpets	Janet Granger
		Tatting Collage: Adventurous Ideas for Tatters	Lindsay Rogers